The Art of the
Gentle Healer

The Art of the
Gentle Healer

A simple story of love, devotion and courage

PETER WRIGHT

iUniverse, Inc.
Bloomington

The Art of the Gentle Healer
A simple story of love, devotion and courage

iUniverse books may be ordered through booksellers or by contacting:

iUniverse
1663 Liberty Drive
Bloomington, IN 47403
www.iuniverse.com
1-800-Authors (1-800-288-4677)

ISBN: 978-1-4620-4767-3 (sc)
ISBN: 978-1-4620-4768-0 (ebk)

Library of Congress Control Number: 2011915131

Printed in the United States of America

iUniverse rev. date: 08/22/2011

This book is dedicated to

That steadfast group of

MENTAL HEALTH THERAPISTS

Who straighten path's

Clear jungles

And work their magic in the minds of

Those in need.

The Art of the Gentle Healer

CONTENTS

Chapter 1

"Each substance of a grief hath twenty Shadows."

William Shakespeare

Those few words by William Shakespeare aptly sum-up the essence of the manner in which the griever is constantly reminded of a tragic loss. Initially as an overpowering force, as though a mighty surf has tossed us up on the strand drained and torpid, and then focused on a loss which, all at once is irrevocable. As time passes, unmeasured and immutable, we are constantly reminded of our loss by near or distant shadows that lurk, like ghosts in clear view; a piece of music, a waft of perfume, a street scene, a mop of straight white-hair in a crowd,or a familiar voice, all will cause a physical tug at the heart and the sharp, stinging reminder of salt in the eye.

*

A year has passed since Gloria died; a tight, timeless year of depressed days. Christmas lost its charm, its intimacy, and became a distant, noisome parody out of sight, almost forgotten by the time new year's cacophony told me that it was *last year* that Gloria had passed on to wherever we go at the end of our life on earth.

And I wonder about that: where do our spirits go? Indeed, the "hereafter" is still a great unsolved mystery to me. There is not a shred of evidence that our spirits go anywhere after we die. The Old Testament seems to me to be a litany of punishment and fear and perhaps the worst literary attempt at an explanation of how our earth was put together, and how we came to live on it.

Nevertheless, in spite of my doubts about facts and definitions put forth by the Prophets and widely relied upon by a large part of our universe, my logical brain tells me that the human being has a divine

1

quality to it. I sense the unmistakable hand of a *Higher Power* in our makeup.

I recently listened to three well known anthropologists discussing anthropogenesis. In particular they argued about why and when during the evolution of mankind our species first walked on two legs. (You may believe the story that God created man from Adam's rib). One of the anthropologists thought that he stood upright in order to see farther; the others, that he might conserve energy. It matters little why, but what does matter is the answer to the question, *"did either creature have a spirit?* The question could be simplified by simply asking at what stage of our evolution we were provided with a spirit?

*

In 1983, I fell in love with a nurse whose influence significantly influenced my life. Contained in the following pages are impressions of the way in which my life subsequently changed. My perceptions of her as a busy wife, and our life at home, but more importantly my own experiences of her palliative power of lessening anxiety, and others' views of her gentle talents of healing the troubled mind.

* * *

Chapter II

The Early Days

Two years earlier, I had become infatuated with one of the stars of the Santa Cruz surfing set, and eventually married the woman. I later found out that both she and I had too many character defects to make the necessary adjustments to continue to live together. It turned out that at about the same time, she concluded that perhaps I was not the catch she originally thought I was, but rather a boring Englishman so unlike the surf-set she had knocked around with for years. We had moved from the Avenues in San Francisco to the sub-tropical beaches of Southern California late in 1980, and found an apartment on the beach. In spite of the seemingly exotic drift of our lives, our togetherness became increasingly separate. I began to feel as though I were a 'Sugar Daddy.'

On the particular day, I was harboring these thoughts and ideas, she had gone to the bank, cleaned out our joint savings, and placed them where I could not get them. Not a large sum of money, but it represented some stability in my life, a sense of which I was painfully short. I became angry for the first time in three years; an emotion that was quite rare in my life. The more I thought about this serious breach in whatever trust was left between us, the more I became convinced that one of us would have to leave.

I had made a prior arrangement with my friend Ian MacDonald to have lunch that day at The Reef, a notorious gathering place not far from the dock area. *My committee* (my mental rationalizing committee) got very busy right away, and gave me permission to make the appointment, and if I had a couple of glasses of wine with lunch—what the Hell—I would be able to handle it. I did, in fact, have three of four glasses of red wine with my lunch; a fatal move for someone who had been sober ("dry") for almost three years, and had a prior miserable history of heavy drinking. But my Committee had done its job well. I had walked into a trap that ensnares millions of would-be recovering alcoholics every day. Just proof that one drink is too much, and a thousand is not enough.

Christmas was just around the corner. I had a good job with a large steamship agency, and even though the pay was slightly less than ample, I was relatively content. A professional sailor and well disciplined in my trade but not my habits, I had many friends on the waterfront and was generally well-thought of.

The results of my drinking wine that day could have been forecast by anyone with an elementary knowledge of the disease of alcoholism—and I was wise enough not to try to fool myself. The act was deliberate and the consequences inevitable—I binge drank for two weeks.

Before abandoning me, my wife called the steamship agency district manager.

"Hi! My name is Wright. My husband works for you, but not at the moment—he's drunk at home. If you want to talk to him, that's where you'll find him."

On the Monday following my party at The Reef, the phone rang about 10.am. It was Tom, my district manager. "Hey, Peter, your wife tells me that you're drinking; true?"

Startled out of my wits at this blatant revelation, I was completely non-plussed as to how to answer. "Er—well Tom—I-er—did have a few bevies on the weekend, but I think I'll be ok in a couple of days," I lied.

"C'mon Peter, I know better than that." He paused. "I know your history but we'll not go there." Another pause. "I'll tell them that an unexpected problem occurred at home and you'll be taking time off to get it all squared away. How is that?" He was right about the problem but I hated the deceit. Nevertheless I was eternally grateful to him.

Toward the second week in January, my attack of craziness began to fade and I was able to call a local hospital and secure a place in its alcohol detoxification ward. I spent two days under the influence of a mild tranquilizer and left the detoxification center for the main program feeling infinitely better. I spent an hour talking to the Chief Counselor. I wanted to get back to work and let my district manager off the hook, but the more the counselor talked to me about myself

4

and where I was with the disease, the more I became convinced that perhaps I needed quiet constructive time to clear my brain. I spoke to my friend in the steamship company, and he agreed to extend my "leave" by two weeks.

Some people call it coincidence; I call it synchronicity. I believe in magnetic attraction. Having read a book which dealt with the *bridge between matter and mind*, by Professor David Peat, a physicist at Liverpool University, I was leaning toward his theory that we humans, because of our chemical make-up, are directly connected to mother earth, which in itself is not such an extravagant statement. Consider for a moment the human spirit, the driving force throughout our lives; where does it go when we die? Most structured religions have taken it for granted that our spirits go either to heaven or to hell, the one, a nice place, the other a very nasty place. At least one religion has added two further places where we might languish after death, purgatory or limbo. Purgatory is a place that ordinary sinners suffer until their sins have been expiated before they are allowed into heaven. Limbo must be the saddest place, for it has been nominated as a place where un-baptized babies go along with all the people who were born before the birth of Jesus Christ, and in Limbo they remain for eternity. Where on earth did these people get such sick ideas?

Think what you may about the foregoing religious alternatives, I will stick to the simplest explanation—we return to mother earth or to that infinite universe and . . . . *what?* So far as I am presently concerned, there is no answer.

*

The alcohol ward into which I was led, was much the same as others I had been obliged to occupy during the previous twenty-or-so years I have been addicted. Would this be my last, I asked myself as I threw my belongings onto the bed, or am I condemned to fail again and again until I become a permanent resident; depressed as I was, I knew I was in the right place, even though I re-lived every moment I had experienced at every other treatment center I had been in. There is nothing very uplifting about twenty-odd drunks in various stages of recovery, except that we were all suffering from the same disease—and not on the street.

The following day, Gloria bustled in and I received a very large jolt somewhere behind my ribs. I eyed her every step for a long as I could without gawking at her; neither did I feel very happy about myself, for in my scrutiny of Gloria there was more than a great deal of interest—and I was still a married man.

I very soon met most of the inmates, and all were run of the mill, except Michael, a lineman for an electricity company. He and I hit it off and both of us thought that "that pretty nurse with the super figure and the short curly hair" was in a class of her own. We liked the way she bantered with her clients. She seemed to be able to touch us all with her words of calm wisdom.

After breakfast on St.Valentines's Day, a few days before I would be released, I found a red rose on my pillow. I quickly hid it lest the rest of the lads see it and give Gloria a hard time, for I was positive that it was she who had placed it there. She had, of course, but she had left one on everyone's pillow. Chagrined and somewhat humbled, I had my first glimpse at the inclusive love she had for all of us.

Later that day, just before she went off duty, I thanked her for the rose and for including all of us in her gesture. Surprisingly she acted shyly, as though she had been caught. She gave me the faintest smile and quickly left.

Two days later, I was discharged from the hospital and went straight back to work. I owed Tom, the district manager one, and even though I was already formulating other work plans for myself, he was off the hook.

The Chinese had just made their bold entry in the maritime trade, and I had been appointed to be a sort of Maritime Ambassador to make sure that our agency would do a first class job. We secured the agency from the communists because of our earlier and successful association as agents for *Sovrybflot,* the Soviet Fishing Fleet.

Chapter III

Gloria stretches her Wings

More with the intention of seeing Gloria than of building a solid foundation for my sobriety, I joined the *After Care* group of individuals from the hospital who met for an hour and a half twice a week, at the hospital in downtown Long Beach. The meetings focused on trying to emulate Bill Wilson's teachings and understanding the message of Alcoholics Anonymous. Gloria was the leader of the group.

She told us a little about her past in Detroit where she was born and brought up, and her early training to become a Registered Nurse. After several meetings, held in the evening between seven-thirty and nine, she lost her first nervousness and warmed up to us. She admitted that she preferred looking after people recovering from drug addiction, including alcohol, than looking after sick people in hospital beds. With a great deal of warm intensity, Gloria explained that when alcoholics "got well" after a hospital stay, they left with too much uncertainty about their future recovery, and were often obliged to return for further treatment. Dealing with the body, she assured us, is not the same as treating the mind, or to put it more succinctly, dealing with addiction.

"Getting to know who you really are is the purpose of After Care. Your disease is purely a mental condition fueled by your intake of alcohol or other drugs; if you continue using you will never get well, and chances are you will end up in an insane asylum where you will most probably die." She looked around to see how her forecast had been received, smiled a little grimly and continued. "But worse than that might be that you might stop drinking, *put the plug in the jug* and leave it at that without working on your behavior and personal make-up. You'll die of boredom, and chances are you'll scare people away." Gloria took another pause and started to pace up and down the platform.

"I'm not sure whether to mention the word God or not," she looked around, "I'll just call him a Higher Power. You all have a Higher Power and in order to become sober, truly sober, you have to find it. In short, you must all rejoin the human race. Forget your old ideas, give up your old pals, pay attention to the spiritual part of you—I don't mean going to church every Sunday—I mean the nicer parts of your being. Smile at people, be courteous to people. I won't go on with the litany because I think you all know what I mean. I have been given a job to do here, and during the next twenty sessions I am going to help you achieve all of those goals." She went and sat down amid some desultory clapping. If no-one else understood what she was getting at, I did. I had examined my own life during her talk—I knew.

*

My first order of work was to initiate a divorce. How do I do that? I asked myself. I had not done this before. I called my wife at her workplace and made some apologies for my recent behavior. I was greeted by a cold silence.

"I don't think that you and I are going to be able to make a go of our marriage." I sounded very nervous and unconvincing. Still the stony silence,

"If you are there would you please say something?" I suddenly got the idea that she was enjoying this. Then I heard her say something to someone else at her work, followed by a short laugh.

That did it. "I know that our marriage is failing and I am going to institute proceedings to end it." I said in the most pompous voice I could muster. I was angry.

"Did you hear that?" I yelled. "We had better get together and talk this over, okay?"

"I'll call you later," She said and hung up.

We met the following day at our apartment. Not, perhaps the best place, but there was some stuff I didn't want her to steal.

She seemed not too put out when I faced her and repeated my idea of divorce. She asked me if I had found another woman. I told her "no." "Why did you steal my money?" I asked bluntly. "We could have worked a fair division. There was no need."

"Because I had an idea you were going to start drinking, and you know what that means for people like us: you'd just disappear with it." She had a point. I had no answer for her. "Well, if you want to separate, we can try that for a while." She looked rather forlorn standing in our living room, but I remembered other spats we had had that had gone rather like this without any subsequent significant change in either of our behaviors.

"Let's not fool ourselves Charlene. We are heading for disaster as it is." I was certain that I was right. "You have Paul living with you so you won't be alone." She seemed to brighten up. Paul, her son from a previous marriage, had inveigled his way into our lives and for the past six months had lived in a sleeping bag on our living room floor. I had mentioned many times to both of them that I wanted him to get a job and move out.

"How about alimony and child support?" I asked, fearing the worst.

Without much hesitation, she shook her head negatively and said, "No thanks. Paul and I will manage quite well." I could see that her face was wet, and for a moment, felt like a Dominican monk may have felt at the inquisition. Then she was gone.

I had a few nasty days after that, and questioned myself more than once about the ethics, honesty and wisdom of my actions.

Three days later, I found a small office manned by a woman, on the same street on which I lived, who undertook the filing of simple straightforward divorces. An hour later, I had filed the necessary papers. She told me that the proceedings would take six months provided there were no complications. A friendly woman about forty, she told me that business was brisk these days. She herself, she confided, had been divorced a year and had not regretted a minute of the time she had spent free to do what she wanted. I took heart.

I was fifty-seven and in fairly good physical shape. My mental condition, however, needed some attention.

By this time I had come to the conclusion that that so far as my present employer was concerned, I was *persona non grata*. I already knew where my future lay. What was I going to do with my time? Working around ships was my life and I loved it. I thought that I'd make a move. I already had my NAMS (National Association of Marine

Surveyors) license. I could go back to sea, but the U.S Coast Guard does not recognize British Ministry of Transport Master's Licenses. I wonder how long it would take to obtain a United States Coast Guard License and could I still do the math? I visited the Captain of the Port, USCG the next day who simply said, "You'd be wasting your time, Peter, plenty of really good jobs here in Long Beach." I knew he was right, so I asked Ian MacDonald if there were any jobs open with the company he worked for. There were, and within a week, I was back at the job(s) for which I seemed to have a natural talent—visiting maritime disasters and reporting to the ship owner, the insurance company or the Protection and Indemnity club (P & I Club,) the nature, cause and extent of damage, and explaining the action taken by the surveyor in order to minimize the loss. The situations in which we surveyors found ourselves, were often dangerous; stranded ships, ships on fire, hazardous cargoes and so on. But the pay was good.

I continued to live in the apartment on 3rd Street and saw my ex wife twice after she had left me. She reiterated that she had no objections to the divorce unless I contested the theft of my savings. It took me no time at all to find out that she had spent it on furniture. I told her that I would not contest the money she stole, adding that I was glad she had spent it well, and that I had plenty more where that came from. I saw her flinch. The second time I saw her was by an invitation to her new apartment a couple of streets away, where she showed me lots of new furniture. Not the kind, I was happy to note, I would have bought.

I gave Gloria a blow-by-blow account of the mini-drama, but she told me in no uncertain terms that this was my business and had nothing at all to do with her.

*   *   *

Chapter IV

I fall in love.

I did my best not to miss any of Gloria's After Care classes, but because of my work there were a few I failed to attend. For these omissions I made a point of apologizing to her. She seemed not to care whether I had been there or not. That upset me, and cooled my interest. I told myself many times each day; *Gloria is about thirty. You are old enough to be her father, you silly old goat—cool it.* Nonetheless, I joined her and quite a few of her colleagues in the local coffee shop after meetings and got to know her a little better. One evening, my heart going twenty-to-the-dozen, I asked her if I could take her to dinner sometime. She rapidly agreed, and a date was made. Not only was I thrilled about her agreement, but at the alacrity with which she did so, I began to harbor romantic ideas.

It was not in my make up to think of myself as growing old—ever. The years went by; incidents in my life happened (I called them 'focal points'); I changed my lifestyle; I changed women partners, but I never thought of myself as being of a certain age and was therefore too young to do something or too old to accomplish something else—until now. The idea gave me food for thought but it did not bother me too much—if I felt okay, then it was okay. It did, however, bother me that she was, as I thought, thirty-seven years younger than I, and greatly relieved when I discovered that the age gap was a mere twenty years.

Our dinner together was not very revealing. She had a hearty appetite but not much conversation. I took her to one of the best burger restaurants in Southern California—Hof''s Hut. She told me that this happened to be her favorite eatery but couldn't afford it. Not once did she indicate that any part of the meal would "put the pounds on." French fries and onion rings disappeared in no time.

To break the ice, I asked her to tell me about where she came from and something about her family. "Well I was born in Dearborn, Michigan. Do you know where that is?"

"Oh, yes," I said, "been there quite a few times; the old Nicholson Steel dock at River Rouge. Discharged coils of steel: Only there a few hours."

"Did you get into downtown Detroit?" she asked. "I guess it's not as nice as some of the places you have been, like San Francisco?"

"Just sailed past the city on our way to Bay City, but I lived in San Francisco for a long time—and I loved it. What about your mum and dad, any siblings?"

"Mom worked in a bank until she hurt her back, fell over a telephone wire or something like that. Dad has been a bus driver and a milkman; he bought shares in the dairy Company and makes his money from that. They were divorced about twenty years ago and live separately. I have a brother, Larry whom I love dearly, and a sister, Charlene who now lives in Los Angeles; she and I don't get on very well Gloria appeared fascinated by my early life, especially when I told her that my mother wanted me to be a priest. She thought that all Catholics were weird, told me that she had been brought up under the Baptist regime, which she admitted she thought was even weirder, and confessed that she didn't have much time for religion. Thinking about her that evening after I got home, I wondered if she was just a very shy woman, but guessed I'd have to find that out in a practical manner, but concluded that she had rather tight personal boundaries. She seemed hesitant about telling me about her family and I spent half the night wondering what it was she hadn't told me. I dropped her off at a condominium in Bellflower which she shared with another woman. I kissed her goodnight, and that was warm and tender.

Our friendship strengthened. We spent more time together having cups of coffee and sharing short breaks during the evenings when I had finished work. Gloria told me that she would not be at the hospital very much longer because its heads of staff had indicated that they would soon close the alcohol unit down: she also wanted to move on and expand in her new career, that of drug and alcohol counselor. Little by little we grew to know and understand each other. We were, after all, individually comprised of two sets of different human elements. Gloria, a thirty—seven year old single woman, a nurse from Michigan who became obliged to move away from home—to Los Angeles, fueled only by her own ambition, meets this fifty-seven year old Englishman, a sailor, who is world traveled and world wise, married and divorced twice, but young in heart and not bad looking—he also has a good job. Many years later a friend of mine, a historian who thought she would like to write Gloria's bio, asked her what she saw in me; what was it that drew her to me and agree to marry me? After a long pause, Gloria said, *"I was really attracted to him. He was a recovering alcoholic; There was something about him I wanted to explore."* The condominium in which Gloria livedin Bellflower, was not far from where I lived. There was a dog, Gloria's dog, gingery in color and built a little like a wolf. She had named him Brattlee—and he hated me. He went out of his way to intimidate me every time I showed up, and that was an easy, and no doubt pleasurable job for him. Gloria took a different, more logical and wicked view, *"Brattle won't bother you if you quit coming around,"* giving me one of her brilliant, impudent smiles. Hearing remarks from her like that, always left a lingering question in my mind—Is she testing me?

One of our favorite weekend pastimes was to pack a lunch and get down to Bolsa Chica Beach, find a place where we might stay all day and get full sun. We would lay there for perhaps four hours before I would go in swimming. She was afraid of the ocean surf and never went further than waist high

"Do be careful Herr Peter," Gloria would say to me every time," (I'm not sure why she added the German "Herr"—perhaps it was because I told her I spoke some German and would teach her someday). "You are not as young as you think. There is a strong undertow."

Without paying much heed to her warning (being an old sailor), I would plunge in and get tossed around by the often—boisterous surf. Once however, I found myself carried helplessly north, toward Long Beach, by a strong two or three knot eddy. After I managed to struggle ashore about two miles from where we were picnicking, I knew where I was, but poor Gloria had no idea. She was frantic and angry and spent time telling me about my stupidity through her tears. I was more careful after that.

In June of 1984, she invited me to spend a spiritual retreat with her in Santa Barbara.

In those days, retreats simply reminded me of those dull, silent days at school where we all kept our mouths shut lest some saint strike us down—but with Gloria? Oh, yes. She told me that they were short of rooms at the retreat center and that we would have to share a room. Well, that was wonderful. It was here that she told me of her plans, her dreams of her on future. She wanted to get her Masters degree in Marriage, Family and Child Counseling. (Now shortened to Marriage Family Therapy-MFT.)

*   *   *

Chapter V

I don't remember exactly when I asked Gloria the question that I truly feared to ask. The idea had started in my mind shortly after we got back from Santa Barbara. I knew I loved her. I had this powerful urge to spend a lot of time with her. She was so *safe;* so *self assured;* so *neat;* so *mature.* For the first time in my life I knew that I wanted her to be my partner for life. I dithered and missed coffee dates. I failed to call her and made excuses for not doing so. What an idiot. Then one day I picked up the phone and blurted it out: "Would you consider marrying me, Gloria?" I could hear her steady breathing, "Do you think I should ask your dad?"

A peal of Gloria's inimitable, captivating laughter nearly deafened me. "Ask my dad? What on earth would you want to do that for? He doesn't give a shit". "Yes I've already considered it. Let's do it soon." And that was that. My neurotransmitters went into high gear, pumping large amounts of *Dopamine* into my brain. I felt ecstatic. Long Beach and the Pacific Ocean took on a new beauty.

The structure and tempo of our daily lives changed dramatically. On September 21, 1984, Gloria enrolled in The California Family Study Center, a college in Burbank, Ca., where she could obtain her Master of Arts in Marriage, Family and Child Counseling. Her plan was to have M.A after name before we got married. In order to provide money during her study time, she worked as a counselor at places like Coast View in Anaheim and Mariposa Women's Center, Orange County. I was earning good money and provided any shortfall. Her daily stint of long hours working and often evening hours of study classes soon began to cause stress. She smoked a lot: said it helped with the stress. I had no complaints about the smoking because I smoked a pipe and had for many years. Her stoicism I admired; never a whimper, never a complaint. I knew I had asked the right woman to marry me. We looked ahead a year and agreed that Saturday June 22, 1985 would be our wedding day.

I started to take more overseas jobs simply for the money. Word of the forthcoming marriage spread like wildfire. We were surprised by how many people in Los Angeles County knew either or both of us.

Looking for a place to live took a great deal of planning and consequently a lot of patience. A couple of blocks south of Del Amo Blvd and not far from Studebaker in a maze of small streets lined with small houses, we found our first residence: 211ᵗʰ Street, Lakewood. It wasn't much of a place but it had hardwood floors. Under a scruffy brown carpet I discovered narrow hardwood floors. Further inspection revealed water stains, which I determined had been left by a resident cat. There were also millions of nail holes, fortunately confined to the floor near the walls. Astonished that anyone would actually deface a hardwood floor, I put the query to our young real estate agent. A man with a sense of humor he suggested that the previous owners may have had an odd view of life and had laid the carpet to cover up the pee stains

The house had been built about the mid-fifties during the post-war depression and, along with a further two hundred or so similar tract homes were simply designed with two bedrooms, a living room with a small kitchen area. They probably went for about $7,500 new;. We finally decided to buy it for $110,000.00, "A bargain," the young realtor beamingly assured us, "and it's in a lovely neighborhood."

The back yard was no more than postage stamp sized, but it contained a riotous fence-hanging bougainvillea with crimson flowers, a very old orange tree, a Brazilian Pepper tree and a Hibiscus tree, which seemed to bloom all year round. The kitchen would need remodeling some time in the near future, and the two bedrooms, small but adequate, were also covered with brown carpeting.

Picking the furniture and curtains took us about a month. We found out that we had pretty much the same taste. Another feature not only of our street but all the adjoining streets, was that they were all lined, both sides, with Jacaranda trees. This rather short tree from Central America, has an abundance of purple/blue vine-like flowers. The trunks of the tree give off a faint sweet smelling fragrance. Walking down these beautifully decorated streets in spring was a unique experience which we were privileged to encounter only as long as we lived in Lakewood. As far as I know, we did not see a Jacaranda tree after 1991, when we moved to Northern California. We did however have a Tulip tree in our front yard in Red Bluff.

Gloria had her dog, Brattlee, who still hated me, while I bought a black and white Springer whom I named Billie, who also became another of Brattlee's enemies. The pair of them eventually teamed up and systematically wrecked whatever Gloria and I had planted. I put some English lavender in, her dog tore it out. No matter how many times I put plants in, that dog would pull them up. One Christmas, several parcels containing gifts from her mum, arrived by mail. Being a good mailman, he decided to hide them from a thieving public, and put them behind the garden gate. Need I tell you what happened? Gloria was first home that night and collected the shredded remnants of books and pullovers. I was not allowed to chastise the perpetrators. They were banned to the laundry room for a week.

Living together was never any problem for either of us. I was brought up a Catholic in an Irish Family and was sent to a boarding school where the monks' aim was to select boys for their seminary. I neither wished to become a priest, much to my mother's disappointment, nor did I fit the type. Soon after going to sea, I gave much thought to Catholic dogma and to some of my experiences at the school. The further I moved away from home and the more I got caught up with men who had never been inside a church yet seemed perfectly sound, honest men—simple men most of them—the more diluted became my Catholic ardor.

Gloria was rather more reticent than I about her biblical and liturgical beliefs. She hardly ever spoke of her experiences as a young Baptist girl with two stern relentless (and hypocritical) German parents who lived by fundamental, sterile rules. I know she rebelled and for a while I believe she harbored a little atheism, not toward God, our creator, but toward god the Baptists' mentor. I enjoy, and still do, interrogating people about their beliefs—in anything: I soon found out that Gloria turned off the subject of her early beliefs and avoided further conversation or interrogation about her youthful life, either in, or outside the church.

I think our first Christmas at 211th Street was a triumph for Gloria. I had never seen her so relaxed and joyful. It dawned on me later that day, how devoted she was to helping people recover from the disease of alcoholism. We invited forty or fifty A.A members to spend Christmas Day with us. The invitation turned out for many of them, to have been a port-in-a-storm, and I saw Gloria paying a great deal of attention to those who were seeing us for the first time. Her eyes were bright, her face one large welcoming smile. The following day, she did not stop talking about the event in general, but mentioned some of the guests by name, whom she declared, needed special attention. I had seen her the day before singling people out and talking earnestly to them. Her attention to their emotional needs, whether they knew they had them or not, brought forcefully to my mind her commitment to her fellow humans.

*   *   *

Chapter VJ

Our Wedding

After more than a year's intensive study, Gloria graduated from Phillips Graduate Institute *(formerly The California Study Center),* Burbank, California with her Master of Arts degree in Marriage, Family, and Child Counseling (MFCC) in May, 1985. At the age of thirty-seven she had met her immediate goal—and was ecstatic. She had no plans to further her professional status, only to be the best counselor she could be. Before she could be eligible to become a Licensed Therapist, she would be obliged to work 3000 hours of internship with whoever would agree to take her on. By the time we left Southern California, she had already whittled those hours down by working as an intern at the Mariposa Women's Center.

Our special day, June 22, 1985, dawned bright and beautiful. The ceremony was held in a small non-denominational chapel and conducted by one of the hospital chaplains who had been in attendance when I was in recovery. Gloria and I had written our own version of the common verbiage normally used. We had added a few succinct phrases of our own, including a line or two from one of John Keats's poem.

> *"A thing of beauty is a joy forever:*
> *Its loveliness increases it will never*
> *Pass into nothingness; but still will keep*
> *A bower quiet for us.*

We had written our own ceremony and given it to the chaplain. He had agreed to read our version.

Gloria was adamant that I agreed not to see her just before the ceremony on our wedding day. I think the real reason was that she was very nervous, but she had also arranged for her picture to be taken.

The wedding dress, made for her mother twenty-five years earlier, fitted her perfectly. Made of off-white satin, floor length with occasional embroidered lovers-knots over the bottom half, it had a fitted slim waist and wrist-length sleeves. Dust-pink, scalloped embroidery shoulder-edge epaulettes and similarly designed lace fittings adorned her wrist and neck—lines, and the hem of the dress. There was no train but there were several pleats in the rear material that made a small bustle. The maid-of-honor, Charleen, her room mate, wore a simple blue silk dress, as did the bridesmaids, her niece, Lisa and my youngest daughter, Hilary

Gloria herself looked radiant. She had purchased a pair of satin slippers because, she said, "I'm gonna be on my feet for a long time." Her recent coiffure was adorned with a miniature—curved bouquet of small-petaled flowers: she held another small bouquet of Gardenias.

Everything went off smoothly until it came time for the minister to read our made up service. Rather than "Oak trees growing up side by side until our separation" he started talking about Snow White and her final meeting with Prince Charming. We knew that nowhere in *our* text had we quoted Walt Disney. Our eyes met and I anxiously looked for signs of panic, but all I saw was the-now familiar glint of mischief. Both well disciplined, we managed to turn our giggles into teary sniffles. The chaplain appeared to be completely unaware of his miniature debacle. During our later years, when times were often tough, a mention of Snow White and her prince would always bring us out of the murk.

We had invited all of Gloria's family, who attended, including her Mum and Dad, partly out of curiosity to view this Englishman with whom Gloria was about to "sail away." I had invited both my American daughters, one of whom, Hilary, arrived and made immediate friends with Gloria's niece, Lisa. The rest of the guests were for the most part our A.A acquaintances.

*

Our honeymoon, we spent at a nice quiet private hotel in New Port Beach

Whenever we both had a free weekend, we made the best of it. During the summer of 1985, we spent four or five weekends in Carmel, a small township on the California coast noted for its fashion shops, pricey Bed & Breakfasts. Long before Clint Eastwood decided to make that beautiful seaside resort his home; its natural ambience attracted all of California and many holiday-seekers from other states to its inimitable beauty. Eastwood, who ran for mayor (and was elected) undoubtedly was an added attraction. He was, of course, a popular figure around town and became more so when he opened up a hamburger deli. One of his movies, *Misty* was shot nearby, naturally adding an extra magnet. In a very modern way, Carmel might be considered quaint, but it was the natural beauty that attracted Gloria and I: the cypress trees, the abundance of gaily-colored flowers which seemed to bloom throughout the winter.

Our days were full of joy and wonder. We absorbed as much history and myth as was offered particularly when visiting the Spanish missions. Even though Gloria had lived in Southern California for twelve or so years, she was still quite unfamiliar with some of the beauty spots. I, who had been to many places all over the world, had never explored the west coasts of Washington, Oregon and California. In fact my knowledge of American geography is, to say the least, scrappy.

But our holidays in England were Gloria's greatest delight. My entire family fell in love with her almost at first sight. My son lived with his wife and son in a small house in Bristol. We made it our second home; indeed wherever they moved, their home became our home. She loved the Cotswold Hills and the picturesque villages built hanging on hillsides, or nestled in valley coves. Being an American, she had some difficulty accepting some of the village names—Stow-in-the-Wold, Chipping Sodbury, Chipping Norton, Little Slaughter, Offenham, and so on. But her greatest wonder was how they became so named. Nothing gave Gloria more delight than to wander through these villages without any real purpose in mind, and simply take in the people and their customs and have a cup of afternoon tea with the accompanying cream scone. I can well remember the afternoon she asked the waitress for a "cup of hot tea."

"Madam," said the waitress a little testily, "we are not in the habit of serving anything *but* hot tea." After a few minutes explanation, we had the expression sorted out and for our naivety got an extra scone each.

Lands End in Cornwall captured her mind too. I have pictures of her at Tintagel, crouching in a wall sconce in King Arthur's Castle. There was half a gale blowing with scud (coastal low clouds) rushing by just a hundred feet above us. The expression on her face told me she was elsewhere; perhaps with Merlin. We spent hours gazing out over the western ocean and at the Longship's Lighthouse around which I had sailed many times during my days at sea. She loved the history of Bristol, a seaport with ingress and egress down the narrow River Avon.

One day we had lunch at the perhaps the oldest pub in England, The Llandogger Trow. In Queens' Square, Bristol, dated 1676, part of Bristol's history.

"What kind of a place is this, Herr Peter?" she asked as we sat in the private lounge, very reminiscent of what it might have looked like three hundred years ago.

"This was the main landing place for the West African slaves. Downstairs in the basement is where they sold them. All those iron ring bolts you can see in the corridor are places where they were shackled."

With eyes like saucers, she asked, "Can we go down into the basement and see,?

I grabbed her hand and led her down the dank, sour smelling stone stairs. "She shivered. "Did they really keep the slaves here.?" She whispered. "It smells—terrible."

I could see that she was impressed with the authenticity of this ancient, but popular monument, but wanted to leave. I had a passing thought: how would she handle the Tower of London?

I told her the history of the last time I saw my dad. "Just down there," I said pointing to Bathurst Basin, an adjoining dock, "my dad's ship used to tie up. He was second engineer of a small coaster called *Alecto*. The ship traded between Bristol, Swansea and Newport, South Wales, and the continent—Rotterdam, Antwerp and Ijmuiden. In 1937, one evening in May, mama took me down to see him off. I think she had a premonition of his forthcoming death." I told her of my visit on board, and an unexpected view I had of my dad from the Engine Room grating, naked on the engine room floor, taking a bath out of a bucket. "That was the last time I saw daddy. His ship was cut in half by a larger steamer off the Hook of Holland, three days later. There were only four survivors."

I felt her fingers squeeze my hand. I knew it went home.

*

After working for a couple of years for the survey company I had joined just before our marriage, I began to realize that my salary didn't quite fit the number of hours I put in each week. Gloria had already complained that our weekends were being ruined by the hours I spent on the docks. After a lot of thought, I decided to beard the lion in his den, and drive north to Marin County and ask him directly for an increase in wages.

I suggested to Gloria that we drive to Sausalito, on the northern side of San Francisco Bay, ostensibly to have lunch and dinner, but in reality so that I could drive thirty or so miles further north to my employers house. I told her my plan. She agreed, rather reluctantly, I thought.

On a blustery cold day, a Saturday, I left Gloria at our motel north of Sausalito telling her that I would be back in a couple of hours, and headed for Novato, a small town farther north. The negotiations were simple but lengthy, and with a hard-nosed Englishman. They took much longer than I had anticipated. At about three in the afternoon I returned to the motel to find a very irate Gloria, fists-on-hips, waiting to do battle.

"Where the heck have you been, Herr Peter? Does this guy live in Oregon? I have been waiting out here in the cold for the last two hours, and by the way have been propositioned twice since you left."

Startled at this revelation, I said "propositioned? Do you mean—like—?" I left the rest of the question unsaid.

"Yes I do mean just that," She replied angrily. "I think this hotel must be one of those "pick-up" places," she went on, "Did you know about this place before.?"

Smarting from the implication, I tried to tell her that I knew of no such place and said I was sorry she thought that way. Gloria quickly regained her composure and apologized for her outbreak.

"Well, herr Peter, did you get what you wanted?"

Very happily I was able to assure her that I had. "I can now deposit twice what I used to each month, beginning next month." I think that some of Gloria's upset was caused by her close exposure to my harsh business world where strong steps have to be taken to get immediate results.

The following year, 1987, the company business fell off, and I had just taken on an assistant, an East Indian, whom I could tell would quickly understand the wrinkles in marine surveying and be a great asset to me. His name was Sajjan; I called him Sam. He had sailed in Indian ships as third mate and a very bright young man. We worked together very well. He was a single man; I therefore took advantage of this and spent many more weekends on the beach with Gloria

Sam proved his worth in no time. Quickly picking up on the rather stilted, legal language, his reports often went in as-is without any additions or corrections from me. We worked together so well that it was with some sadness that after a year I had to tell him that I was seriously thinking of leaving the company and going out on my own. My sixty-fifth birthday was a little over a year away, and I knew that Gloria really wished me to retire at that age. Even though I was as fit as ever, I knew that my reactions were not as sharp as they had been two years ago. I agreed with her, hence my advice to Sam. I told him I would recommend that he take my place as senior surveyor. Sam's dismay matched my nervousness. He wanted to join me but he knew that in a "one man business" there is only one man.

In July, I told my boss that three months hence I would be leaving the company and working on my own out of my own office. He was not happy. Gloria, also, was not too happy.

"More work for you, Peter and full responsibility." I agreed with her but explained that I would be able, most of the time, to control my own hours; also I would not be splitting my income.

I know that Gloria watched me very carefully from the moment I went out on my own until I went into hospital with chest pains—coronary artery disease.

My new business mushroomed overnight. Fortunately the appointments were evenly spaced so that I found myself only occasionally tripping over my own feet. One afternoon I met one of the Pacific Maritime Association's (PMA) arbitrators on board a ship.

"How's it going Peter? "she asked me, "I hear you have gone out on your own. Congratulations."

"So far, so good" I replied. "Nothing has arrived on my desk that I can't handle."

"Say, Peter," she went on, "I was talking to George (the PMA arbitrator) Pacific Maritime Association, a short while ago, and mentioned you as a possible relief arbitrator for five or six days each month, while he takes some leave. What do you think?"

"Of course I will," I said without giving the assignment a moment's thought.

"Oh, good," she said, "Would you be good enough to come around to our office tomorrow morning about ten so that we can give you the in's and out's."

I already knew what kind of a job it was—tough! At any time work was being performed on the docks by longshoremen or warehousemen, and a question of health and safety arose, usually instigated by one of the I.L.W.U, (International Longshoreman's and Warehousemen's Union), an arbitrator was called to visit the site and decide if, in his opinion, the complaint was valid or not. The arbitrator's decision was final and the longshoremen were ordered back to work or a hearing was prescribed for a later date.

That evening during the course of conversation with Gloria, I made one of my famous "Oh, by the way . . . ." statements, and told her of my new job. I remember that she was writing at the table at the time. She instantly put down her pen and came over to face me.

"Tell me about this new job again, Herr Peter." I knew she was upset, and I knew why.

"Well, sweetheart,: I began timidly, "it's not really much of a job—and the money is good." I got no further.

"It'll buy a really nice coffin for you, I suppose," she said. There were tears in her eyes. "We have enough money now, don't we? What is it with you and money?"

The question didn't startle me, but it brought back to mind my nightmarish ghost of being penniless. I had already told Gloria of my alcoholism and my descent to its depths. The following is a summary of the nature of that Chimera.

Ever since I had ended up penniless and homeless on Market Street, San Francisco in 1978, I have had an issue about financial insecurity.

I remember well how my mother took the helm after my father lost his life, and how she fought the courts for the smallest financial compensation. How lovingly she looked after us kids and provided for us. At the age of forty, she went out and got a clerks job at the Bristol Aero plane Company, and became our lifesaver and hero through five and a half years of war. When she died in 1961 it was as though my very foundations had crumbled, and even though I had a first mate's job at that time, my mind took me to a time, somewhere in the future, when I might find myself on my own, homeless and penniless. I knew that I didn't have my mother's courage, and the blind fear that I might end up destitute on the streets of some city lingered with me, like "Banquo's Ghost" did with Macbeth. That paranoid memory turned into reality in March 1978, when I found myself on skid row in San Francisco.

* * *

Chapter VII

Retirement

I had had several summons's to the docks to settle disputes, and so far had not experienced any serious one's, but I found the job stressful. I am certainly not the kind of person who "gives and takes" when there is a black and white decision. If, in my opinion, there was no health and safety issue, then that was that. There were no 'ifs, ands, or buts. But it was hard on my nerves.

At two o'clock one morning in October 1987 the telephone at my bedside rang. A voice announced that there was a labor dispute and stoppage in Wilmington, and would I kindly attend. For the first time in my life I felt my heart speed up and I noticed that I was short of breath. Breathing heavily, I pulled on my clothes.

"Are you okay, Peter? You are breathing hard." Gloria turned over in bed and grabbed my jacket. I can't remember what I said, but tried to reassure her and left for my car. On the way down the street, I felt woozy and light headed. As I got to the end of the street I saw five or six motorcyclist, pulled over, sitting on their bikes. Druggies, I thought. All stared at me as I passed. At about this time I decided that it would be foolish for me to continue to Wilmington, and instead of turning onto the next street, made a "U" turn and headed back down my street. As one, the motorcyclists revved their engines and roared off. A busted drug deal, I thought. Surprised, too, for I thought we lived in a drug-free neighborhood.

Gloria was at the front door when I got out of the car, dressed and ready to go.

"Don't turn the engine off Peter, get out and sit in the passenger seat." Twenty minutes later I was in the Emergency Room of Long Beach Hospital. Scared, and wondering what it was like to die, I hadn't uttered a sound since she started driving.

Gloria was back in her realm. Her last three years at Ford Hospital in Detroit had been in the E.R. I no longer felt sick, in fact I felt okay, and had the temerity to tell Gloria.

"Try and act responsibly, Peter. This is no joke. Do exactly what you are told and don't try to be a smart-ass."

Later on that morning, they went into an artery near my groin and performed an angiogram. They found two of the small arteries on the left side of my heart to be eighty per-cent occluded. They explained that they were blocked with plaque, the result of high fatty cholesterol, and that under circumstances where the arteries were more occluded (blocked) the artery would burst and that would be called a heart attack probably resulting in my death.

Surgery was done two days later. They removed two veins from my left leg and used what they needed to repair the two clogged arteries.

Gloria turned up morning, noon and evening: no flowers (at my request), but with a wealth of encouragement and common sense. I spent about twelve days in Long Beach Community Hospital and made friends of the Cardiologist, a Polish doctor, who told me in straight language how to recover from the surgery. The surgeon, whose name I forget, was precise with his knife and left scars that became invisible after six or seven years.

From my hospital bed I called P.M.A and asked them to make other arrangements for a relief arbitrator; perhaps my greatest gift on returning home.

Now that I had some free time, I decided to make a list of improvements Gloria and I wanted to make. The list was long and expensive, but something we could afford, and I would not be capable of doing myself was to install in our tiny backyard, a patio—a concrete patio, over which I would lay tile when I became fit. Saturday's paper showed an ad for someone who did just what we wanted. We called the number and the person who answered sounded Hawaiian. He told us that he'd be up the following day to look the job over.

To our surprise, the man who turned up was a very large Samoan, in national costume. He assured me that the job was simple and would take a week, and the cost would be $200.00 in total. It was a Saturday, my last weekend off, so we arranged for him to arrive with his equipment at eight on the following Monday morning.

By seven o'clock on Monday morning, I was on the waterfront testing out my heart and Gloria was at home when he arrived in a beat-up Toyota truck towing a cement mixer. To her surprise he had brought his wife and another Samoan of almost equal physical proportions to her husband. He explained that he never left his wife at home because he thought that Hawaiian Gardens, the city in which they lived, was dangerous. He said she, his wife, would clean the house for us at no extra charge. Being Gloria, she saw no harm in this offer, and agreed.

That day we had lunch at the Marriott at the end of the wharf. She seemed somewhat uneasy about the arrangement at home and said she would stop at the house on her way to work. Half an hour later she called me. "Herr Peter," I could hear the panic in her voice, "you'd better come home; I think we are in a lot of trouble."

"What? What's going on?" I too was filled with unknown horrors.

"The house is filled with kids. It looks as though the man who was doing our cement has brought his whole family; they are all over the house." Her voice was decidedly panicky.

I was already closing my office down for the day. "What did they say when you told them to leave?"

"They just smiled." I heard her sigh. It didn't sound too desperate to me.

There were two vehicles in front of the house when I got home, the old beat-up Toyota truck, and an equally dilapidated small Ford. Toys of every description littered our tiny front lawn. Gloria was at the front door, a glimmer of a smile on her otherwise calm face.

I walked through the house into the back yard and singled out our large Samoan, busy with the concrete mixer.

"I didn't get your name the other day. What is it?"

"They call me Hank," he said brushing his hands off on his pants, "my real name is Pontaloa." A large, disarming smile transformed his face.

"Okay Hank," I spoke gently, "who are all these children and why are they here?"

Scratching his cement filled hair he smiled and looked vaguely over my shoulder. "Well sir, my wife looks after kids of other wives whose husbands have to work. My wife goes with me everywhere 'cos I don't trust her at home by herself. So she brings all the children. They are all good children and my wife will punish any who are bad—or break anything." He looked at me for my reaction.

"Just a minute Hank." I said "Let me talk to my wife."

On my way to find Gloria I met "Mrs. 'Hank, a handsome island girl of about twenty-five, surrounded by eight children all gazing at me with big round eyes. It seemed that Gloria had corralled them from the bedroom and bathroom and told their keeper to restrain them until I arrived.

I explained to Gloria their reason for being at our house, and knowing that this was a sensitive incident, asked what she thought about it.

"It's not that I don't trust them: I don't know them," she said after a moment, "and I do understand why Hank doesn't want to leave her on her own all day. She can't just abandon them, and in a sense we can't abandon them. Hmm!"

Gloria went over to Mrs. 'Hank,' took her by the hand hand, led her to the sofa and told her to sit down. The kids crowded in behind their 'mom.' I watched as Gloria began to talk to her. I didn't hear all of what she said, but the gist of her talk was that she, Gloria, fully understood her predicament and under the circumstances was prepared for her to bring along whatever kids she had to look after each day provided that she, the 'mom,' kept them entertained, busy and fed. She further explained that this kind of practice was not acceptable here in the United States and she urged that she talk to her husband and try to persuade him to let her stay at home with the children. The woman nodded frequently as though she understood, and half an hour later, at the end of the day, the entire family left.

I had the usual questions; how she felt about the entire episode and so on, but I had nothing but admiration for the way Gloria had handled the situation. She decided to put her trust in another complete stranger. Later in her career, her charisma, and skills in inviting her clients to 'tell all, won her a vast amount of respect and confidence.

The cement job was finished on time and to my satisfaction; our house had been cleaned and nothing had been stolen.

* * *

Chapter VIII

House hunting again

Gloria and I talked at length about my retirement. After my heart surgery she became pretty adamant that I retire as soon as my Social Security payments took effect; on my birthday in 1991 when I would be sixty-five.

My health had improved greatly. We were both eating well, and exercise was part of our daily routine. I still swam in the ocean without being a foolish landlubber. I was probably as healthy as I had ever been and was inclined to overdo it. I secretly decided that I would work until I was seventy, and if nothing changed, I would stay another five years. I really loved the job I had and had earned a reputation in London, New York and of course Los Angeles/Long Beach.

I had not taken into account my reaction time in dangerous situations. I had a phone call one morning around Easter, 1991 and learned that one of my colleagues had been killed earlier that day. It appears that he was in a self operated hydraulic lift inspecting the internal condition of a set of folding, steel hatch covers. The crew had inadvertently moved the steel hatch covers while he was at the top of the lift, and crushed his skull. He died instantly: the incident shook-up all of us surveyors. My thoughts were directed toward his last living seconds and if a second's faster reaction would have been enough to avoid the accident. None of us, of course, will ever know; but the thought stayed with me. One morning later in the same month, I had descended into the cargo hold of a vessel discharging bundles of steel pipe in one-ton bundles. As I ascended the vertical steel ladder to exit the hold, one of the wire slings of a large load of steel pipe being hoisted ashore, probably seven tons in weight, slipped, causing the entire sling—load to swing toward me. The end of the sling-load struck the bulkhead with tremendous force about twelve inches to the right of my torso, causing a two inch dent in the bulkhead. I did hear the longshoremen yelling at me, but since I was partially hidden from their view, it didn't really matter.

It was then that I had an epiphany, and realized that my reactions were not what they used to be, but most of all about I criticized my own lack of judgment—and complacency. I should have waited for that sling to have cleared the hold before attempting to exit. I had committed an error that might have ended my life.

I told Gloria that evening that I would retire on my birthday, a few months away—and hoped that I would make it. I did not tell her what had caused a reversal of my original plan. She was very happy.

Christmas 1990, was a huge affair. My friend Ian, who confided in me that he was leaving the area and trying his hand as a surveyor in Houston, had rented the lobby of a nearby hotel and instructed the manager in detail what was to be laid out in the way of main and side dishes. The main attractions were two larger platters each containing baked, wild salmon and all the trimmings. The side dishes were shelled oysters, steamed mussels, New Zealand lamb and a side of beef, every vegetable one could imagine, and several English Style Christmas cakes and six Christmas puddings all stuffed with dimes. (It was customary years ago to bake the Christmas Puddings with a quantity of three-penny bits in it; about the same size as a dime). Naturally alcohol was served in every form. Ian was quite a remarkable character; he could play the guitar well and could imitate Elvis Presley well enough to hold his audience.

Even though Gloria shied away from big events, declaring that her shyness singled her out as a 'wallflower,' I noticed that after she had been at any function for thirty or forty minutes, her shyness developed into a certain hesitant charm. People began to like her, and most people who hung in with her, ended up loving her. I think it was part of her defenses; a sort of test on her part to ensure that whomever she was talking to, was *'safe.'*

A couple of years later, after we had made a trip to Detroit to see her folks, I detected certain hostility during her conversations with her parents. Not really obvious but subtle innuendoes. If the conversation drifted into finances, theirs or ours, Gloria would almost bristle. I questioned her about her attitude when we got home and became aware that she had no great love for either of her parents. Her father, it seems, had been a cold disciplinarian, without a generous atom in his body. I found him boring and apathetic. He appeared to lack any parental emotion toward his children; never once hugging or kissing them. As time went by, they became even farther distanced. Gloria remembered every holiday and his birthday and sent him an appropriate card. One card each year, would arrive from him demonstrating the state of stagnation he had reached: a Christmas card with his name under the commercial greeting and a ten dollar bill. It seemed to me that if the money was supposed to be a gift, then it had become an insult.

Gloria and her mother had a warmer relationship, which grew even warmer as time went by. Betty Aeilts,who had divorced her husband many years beforehand, was inclined to be narcissistic and a hypochondriac. She considered herself to be a cut above the rest of society, particularly her husband. The filial love Gloria had for her mother appeared to me to be cyclic. One of the major reasons Gloria harbored a resentment toward both her parents was because, while at high school, neither of them showed the slightest interest in what she intended to do with her life. In every respect but one; From an outsiders point of view, Harold and Betty Aeilts appeared to be ideal parents. They looked after the three children well enough during their school years, but interest in their welfare appeared to dry up when they had all graduated. Each of them fended for himself after graduating from high school. Without any encouragement or assistance, Gloria saw herself through Nursing School and became a State Registered Nurse without so much as a *Hurrah!*.

When the time came for her to move on, she had no qualms leaving both her mom and dad in Michigan. There was an obvious lack of affection in the Aeilts family.

*

Both Billie, my Springer, and Brattlee, Gloria's Wolfhound, became ill during the early part of 1991. Billie contracted tetanus through eating infected local dirt. Apparently, prior to our housing development, all of the land had been dairy farmland.

Brattlee, unfortunately, being of lupine origin, developed dysplaysia. Billie survived, but Brattlee eventually lost the use of his back legs. Poor Gloria was heartbroken. She knew what was going to happen to him.

Gloria and I had often discussed moving away from the Los Angeles area; we both favored Northern California or Oregon. Knowing nothing about our neighboring state, we persuaded a real estate person who lived just south of Portland to look after our interests. This she did admirably, and sent us details of several promising looking houses, but she was failed to tell us about places where Gloria might practice her therapy. She named a few hospitals but Gloria shuddered at the thought of working in or anywhere near a hospital. They were anathema to her.

For Gloria, the prospect of leaving Lakewood proved daunting. On the one hand, traveling into new territory looking for a place to live, smacked of the days of the settlers, and the places we intended to look sounded like gold mining towns. But she had strong ties to southern Los Angeles County; she had many friends whom she would greatly miss.

For me, it would be the end of an era. I had no such ties to those with whom I had worked. I might miss the excitement of a new, important job; I would miss the ocean and Bolsa Chica Beach. What struck me most of all was that I was the last of the seafarers in my family. My brother, a Chief Officer in the Union Company, had recently died in Australia, and the Rodger's, my mother's Irish family, were all in Davy Jones' Locker. I did not, however, mourn the occasion because seafaring had changed dramatically since I first went to sea at age seventeen. Containerization (stuffing cargo of every description into steel containers and stowing these articulated steel boxes in specialized slotted holds) was here to stay, even though I was quoted at one time, as having declared the container to be a future maritime disaster. Thousands of containers have been lost overboard as a result of heavy weather. The computer, incapable of dealing with the ships' behavior at sea, is very proficient at placing them on board. Those irretrievably lost over the side are all out there in mid-Pacific somewhere, bobbing about, if they have sufficient buoyancy or resting on the bottom, still full of television sets, or cameras. I suppose the insurance companies can deal with the loss. I don't know.

But first we had to find a place to live, and that we decided would be during the late winter or early spring of 1991.

*   *   *

Chapter IX

We find a home in a Cowboy town

In late February or early March, we drove north in our pale blue Honda Civic. We decided to drive north on Highway.101, until we left Carmel, then drive east to Interstate.5.until we found a house or a location we would like to live in.

Taking the Pacific Coast Highway in Long Beach, the drive north through Oxenard and Ventura became an endless view of shabby houses and broken fences until we got to Santa Barbara where we stopped for lunch and found lots of red tile roofs, portico's and bougainvillea; stately, wealthy homes. We stopped at all the well known beaches, Pismo Beach, famous for its clams, and Grover Beach, famous for—something! And then Cambria, a strange, small town, which became famous when film starts gathered there every so often to indulge in what might be described as *risque* behavior. The large art-deco houses are all named after the stars of the time: Charlie Chaplin, Mary Pickford and Douglas Fairbanks.

Onto Morro Bay,which reminded me of an overgrown beach holiday resort with blue and white painted beach houses scrambled on top of each other. Finally we drove into Carmel-by-the-Sea, our little heaven on earth. We stayed at the same B & B that we always had, owned and run by a very uptight German gentleman, who reprimanded me about my smoking. I had smoked a pipe for years and thought nothing of producing my pipe whenever I felt like it. He caught me smoking on the patio and, very respectfully said, "Excuse me, Herr Wright," he coughed lightly as though my smoke had caught him in the throat, "there may be guests in my establishment who cannot inhale tobacco smoke, and may come after me and complain. Would you, therefore, be kind enough not to smoke under my roof?" How could I refuse his request?

After two heavenly days doing absolutely nothing but hold hands and grin at each other, and meander along the beaches picking up stones and sea shells, we headed back to the main highways 5 and 80 north stopping at Sacramento to see the historic part again and take another look at the famous railway museum. The most fascinating part of the Railway Museum for me was the simulated movement of the carriages as if they were on a transcontinental run. With the whistle blowing and the *click-click—clak-clack* of the wheels hitting each joint in the rail, I could well have been on the overnight express to Chicago—very romantic.

We decided to stop at Red Bluff, probably because of the name; a town of some 10,000 souls. The Sacramento River, which rises in the Siskyou mountains, and becomes a sizeable stream at Redding and a moderate river at Red Bluff, was navigable to the latter named town. All timber and building products for houses and other structures in Sacramento and San Francisco traveled by river steamer directly south to both ports. Redding, a city of 100,000 souls, lies thirty miles north.

The first exit to Red Bluff is marked as Main Street, and if you stay on it, you'll find yourself back on Interstate 5 five minutes later, headed north. It was about noon when we got there and we were hungry. Before we stopped at a sandwich shop on Main, we drove up and down some of the streets adjoining Main, streets with original names like Washington, Franklin, and Jefferson. (and so on). There were quite a few picturesque, stately Victorian houses, some in good repair, some not so attractive, but there was nothing that looked like a place we would choose to live in. Victorians, although romantically and architecturally desirable, are prone to serious latent defects such as one-hundred-year-old plumbing and eighty-year-old electric systems. Before dark, we drove out of Red Bluff with the sense that we had never been there. We took away with us no memories of quaintness, beauty or, indeed—anything.

Our next and as it turned out, our last northbound call, was Redding. Once again we went on an unguided tour of six or seven housing developments, none of which appealed to either of us. There were views of Mount Lassen and Mount Shasta from some of the sites we visited, but the appeal of a mountain view failed to overcome the drabness of the buildings we were looking at. We discussed driving to Oregon, south west of Portland where we had originally set our sights, but it would have added about one thousand miles to our trip, and promptly dismissed the idea.

On the way south, we stopped at Red Bluff again. We thought that perhaps we'd contact a real estate person and get shown around, especially since Redding appeared barren. Stopping at the same sandwich shop, we ordered one of their special sandwiches and talked about what kind of place we were really looking for. A well dressed, good looking woman sitting at an adjacent table leaned over and told us that she was a real estate agent and that she asked us to forgive her for eavesdropping, but she thought she might have just the place we were looking for. Her name was Cheri Poulson. She was having lunch with another lady, another Real Estate agent, and her good friend named,Joanne Perkins.

She explained that her uncle had a two bedroom, one and a half bath, large living room, dining area bungalow sitting on two acres—with almond trees. I suppose it was the acreage that caught our attention. We had often agreed that a couple of acres would make us landowners—and what could we do with it? Horses; goats; perhaps a couple of sheep?

The house, situated on the west side of Wilder Road, lay between two similar houses, amply screened from each other by tall trees and dense hedges and set back off the road about 30 feet: a dream home for two naive city folk. Two well-tended acres stretched out back with thirteen almond trees on it. Not prepossessing specimens of that particular species of nut tree, but we were assured that almonds appeared every year. The vegetable and rose gardens were pretty well tended. Several cherry trees, we were informed, gave a bumper crop each year.

The owner wanted to close escrow around July/August, months that suited us well, provided no spanners fell into the works. We made a deal there and then, said goodbye to our real estate angel and drove back toward Los Angeles and Lakewood.

*   *   *

37

Chapter X

Reflections on our Future

Just before my sixty-fifth birthday, Gloria announced that she had worked the required number of supervised hours and would be taking her Boards Examination within the next two weeks. So much was going on at once, that we had a hard time keeping our calendars straight. We had already decided that following the State Boards Examination, whether she passed or failed, we would leave southern California for our home in Red Bluff, but I hasten to add that failing the exams never entered my mind. Gloria was a winner. I knew that with all the studying she had put in, and the confidence she talked about her job I knew she would come through with her mainsail full and taught

The examinations were to be held in a hotel in Sacramento. We drove down to the capital the evening before and attempted to lead an ordinary, casual evening, but all we did was chatter and reassure each other that tomorrow would be just fine. This was to be an oral exam during which she would be confronted with a vignette or two, containing a real life situation: a family circumstance in which drugs or alcohol, children, a partner breakup, or one of the many individual or marital occurrences that happen daily, would be presented to her for her evaluation and solution. The exam would last an hour.

A week beforehand, Gloria had visited JC Penney and bought herself a skirt, blouse and shoes. She put them on for the first time a few hours before walking into the exam room. I had never seen her dressed up in colors before, and she was radiant. A white edge-to-edge silk blouse with petite-pointe embroidered knots around the cuffs and at the base of close fitting, buttoned collar. The cotton skirt reminded me of one of Monet's pictures, pale blues, poppy reds and touches of other pastels. Her shoes were very fashionable two tone satin covered, medium heel.

Standing in front of the mirror twisting and peering, she asked, "Herr Peter, are my boobs too big? Does my ass stick out too far? How about my cleavage? I tried to imagine how she felt. I kind of knew where she was coming from, from my own experience when I went up for my Masters Orals at Cardiff not so long ago. I suggested a small change here and there, but as far as I was concerned, she looked nothing less than gorgeous.

I waited in the lobby more anxious than I would have believed. Finally she stepped out of the elevator beaming all over her face. We did one of those movie embraces much to the delight of the onlookers. I could feel her trembling with relief and pure joy. She was also very proud of herself. All her perseverance and hard work without any financial help had now paid off. Poised at the threshold of her career, she was thirty-seven years of age.

I had reached a stage in my life where people of my age say to themselves, "I have worked forty-eight years of my life and I think that I have earned the right to stop work and take it easy—enjoy the rest of my life without feelings of guilt." For some reason or other, probably the manner in which I was brought up combined with my genetic make-up, I had no such thoughts. My energy level was high, I did not feel as though I was sixty-five, I was a professional seafarer and had no hobbies, and I wanted to go on working. But what struck me mostly about this particular phase of our lives, Gloria's and mine, was that at exactly when I was stepping away from the helm of our little ship, she was just about to start her career. Was she going to take over the steering of our ship? Up to this moment, six years after our marriage, I had never thought of our future in such black and white terms. Indeed, I had never thought of my future in these terms at any time during any of my previous three marriages. What was it about this woman, Gloria, that gave me pause for this ambivalence?

I knew that the tasks for which she had just been qualified, were her own and no-one else's. They were private to the outside world; confidential in nature and of which I would never be part. She was on her own. For her profession, and in many ways, her personal support, she would rely on that of her colleagues.

And that was how it worked out.

Chapter XI

The Outcasts of Poker Flat

We started eying our belongings, wondering what we should sell, take with us or abandon. We really hadn't given a great deal of thought about what kind of furniture we should have in a house on the outskirts of a cowboy town. In the end, we decided not to change our lifestyle radically, but to take all of our goods and chattels and be comfortable. Neither of us could imagine living in a house with bent willow furniture and a bed made of lodge pole pine. The night time serenade of the numerous packs of coyotes was enough westernizing for us; something we hadn't bargained for.

The spring and summer went by fast and for both Gloria and me, a very busy time.

At the beginning of June 1991, I received a phone call from local lawyers representing a European steamship company, with instructions to attend on board a large bulk carrier that had collided with a large tanker just outside Los Angeles harbor limits. And would I kindly attend on board the tanker in order to get the Masters' opinion. The following day I had another call with instructions to take charge of the investigation of a ship calling at Los Angeles as a Port of Refuge: her cargo of coal was smoldering. The owners of the ship with the hot coal had declared General Average, a rather complicated business where all parties interested in the particular voyage, agree to pay for the total loss in accordance with each of their singular interests in this particular voyage.

Fortunately, the master of the oil tanker outside Los Angeles harbor refused, peremptorily, to allow any investigators on board and sailed a day or so later. One less job for me, for which I was truly thankful.

The ship that had been in collision with the oil tanker came alongside. Divers discovered a ten-foot gash in the shell plating below the waterline in way of No.4.hold thus confining the area affected by the ingress of sea water The ship was loaded with bulk cement. The cement was discharged from No.4 hold, the salvageable portion was finally reloaded; the unsalvageable cement was set aside on the dock and every attempt was made to sell it.

The ship with the hot coal came alongside and the it was unanimously agreed to discharge the entire cargo, 80,00 tons The good coal was segregated from the hot and after forty days the ship sailed for China leaving behind two or three thousand tons of coal which had by now become less lethal and was eventually sold to local interests

*

Meanwhile, Gloria continued to work at the Mariposa Women's Center, not as an intertern but as a staff member. She was well liked as a woman with a great sense humor,

And greatly respected for her counseling skills.

As our departure from Lakewood became imminent, I met socially more and more with her co-workers. I could see how and why they were going to miss her. More than anything, I think they were going to miss her infectious laugh or trill, a noise she managed to produce that sounded like two tones trying to escape from that place where she stored her risible faculties—her irrepressible humor.

*

We consigned our furniture to one of the big household goods carriers. The driver informed us that he would deliver our goods to Red Bluff a week hence. He explained that he had another pick-up and a delivery in Sacramento before he headed north.

Before we drove away from our little house on 211th street we had to deal with our two dogs, 'Billie' had overcome the effects of tetanus, but 'Brattlee' could barely stand. If he fell into the splayed position he was unable to get up.

Poor Gloria became depressed and tearful as the day of our departure approached. Unknown to me, she had called a veterinary surgeon on Clark Avenue and made arrangements for him to be put-down at 09.30 the following day.

"He'll never be able to make it as a normal dog in Red Bluff," she sobbed, "and he'll never be able to fool around with 'Billie" She hardly slept a wink that night.

At 09.15 we left Lakewood. As we turned on Clark Avenue, she pulled over to the curb and said, "Please stay in the car: I have something to do." Wondering what she was up to, I watched her get out and open the rear passenger door, reach in and lift 'Brattlee' out. Gathering his lead in one hand she stumbled into the Vets' surgery. I knew what was happening, but I had no idea that she had planned it for today.

How am I going to handle this? How was Gloria going to be when she returned? I had no idea that this is what she had on her mind I nodded agreement. Ten minutes later she silently got into the car and we drove off. We didn't speak for a long time, each of us quietly remembering her friend. 'Billie' Joined us in our lamentations and whimpered for the next couple of hours.

We took the fast route north and both breathed a sigh of relief when we got to the top of the Grapevine. The day was a typical August day in Southern California. The Sacramento valley spread out before us displaying its enormous wealth and abundance of vegetables, made us almost simultaneously realize that we had left behind the smoky horrors of "civilization" and were about to embrace real America—and real Americans.

We both cheered up and celebrated our arrival in rural California at a small greasy spoon in Lamont at the bottom of the Tehachapi grade. We were, however. to have our eyes opened with some rural set-backs.

We checked on our house and found the present owner having a garage sale. I bought a beat-up sit-on mower for an exorbitant price, and asked him to recommend an inexpensive Motel. Without hesitation he said, "Oh, The Flamingo is cheap; at the far end of Main Street.".

Dutifully, stupidly we sought the Flamingo Motel and found a run-of-the-mill, rather dingy place guarded by two enormous wooden flamingoes perched on the lawn out front. The room we rented smelled of God-knows-what, there were cockroaches and spiders, which, for most people, are an anathema; for Gloria they are a total abomination. I wasn't too happy either. The manager, a tough looking cowboy type female, heard our complaints with a stony face. "Cockroaches won't hurt you, neither will ants. I can give you a can of "Raid" and they'll be gone in a flash." I'm sure she was hoping that these two city sissies would not bother her any more. She probably had a hot date somewhere. "Won't hurt you," she indignantly replied, "I can give you a can of ant spray if you like," she said.

Dead beat, we decided to stay the rest of the night and spent our first night in a town we had decided to settle down, watching black and white war movies. Our suitcases remained closed. The following morning we left money at the front desk to cover our stay and went to have our first breakfast in Port of Red Bluff.

At some time that morning, we spoke to our real estate agent. She told us that the house was now empty, and would we like to see it? While we were looking our new home over, Cherry, our estate agent, told us the bank wanted to check out a few things, and would we call them.

The person looking after our loan touched on a few of the answers we had provided on our application. She was talking to Gloria. "So, your husband is retired?"

I could see Gloria's eyebrows twitch. "Yes. Why?"

". . . . and you, Mrs. Wright, work at The Mariposa Women's Center . . ."

Gloria interrupted her. "No! No! Do you think I'll be commuting to Orange County every day? No, I left them a week ago."

"So you are unemployed and your husband doesn't work: is that right? Then I suggest that your loan is suspended."

Gloria's face had assumed a color I'd never seen before; a bright pink, and her eyes had become steely.

"Get me your supervisor please . . . No, I shall not wait just a minute. Please get me someone else on the line; someone who knows about moving from one end of the state to the other." She covered the mouthpiece and said some things that I dare not repeat, words that were frequently used on the waterfront.

A few minutes later she was talking to someone else. The gist of her conversation was that she, Gloria, had just obtained her Master of Arts degree and was about to launch her career in northern California. She would serve the community in which she resided, and explained that there were many other services with whom she could work.

At the end of the discussion, the loan was not suspended. We breathed collective sighs of relief. Gloria muttered about the stupidity of this bank for the next few days.

As promised our household goods arrived on time. By nightfall, we were pretty well organized. The garage, as it is supposed to be, was full of boxes and the things we were going to "find a place for" later on. At a rather late hour we decided to quit and I went out to close the garage door only to discover, with a little humor mixed with my amazement and irritation, that there was no garage door. It seemed to me, after a cursory inspection, that there never had been a door. Gloria had to come and see for herself and promptly collapsed laughing uncontrollably. Even though it was well after eleven I had to call the previous occupant.

"Hey. Les! Were you aware that there is no door to the garage?"

"No door? Well . . . er . . . there never was one. You city folk are too cautious. No-one steals stuff—like furniture or household property around here."

"Then why have you got two dead locks on your front door and a window jammer in the living room"?

A silence lasted five or so seconds. I could hear his heavy breathing and almost hear his mind trying to think of an answer. At last he said, "We did have a scare once . . ."

"I'm going to charge you for a new door and an opener." I said by way of a "good night."

Once again I heard Gloria muttering to herself and giggling, *"No garage door!"*

As we closed up the house for our first night in the 'wild west,' I thought of communities such as this, with which I admit I had never been shipmates, but wondered at the comment made by our departed ex-owner, that there was no thievery in Red Bluff.

I called out to Gloria, already snuggled down in bed, "Maybe you already have a couple of ready-made clients."

"What did you say, Herr Peter?" I repeated my rather disagreeable comment. She didn't say anything but gave me one of her more dismissive looks. It warned me not to be unkind.

*

Billie, our Springer, loved the open spaces where he could chase quail and rabbits. During the not-too-hot evenings, Gloria and I took him around a large piece of land to our west, perhaps ten acres. While he did his Billie things, we collected wild flowers we had never seen or heard of. One we found in a shaded stream bed was called a Peruvian Lily, a beautiful cluster of purple and white trumpet-like flowers. Beneath a mulberry tree in our garden here in Redding, they appear every April reminding me of other times in another world. Wherever Gloria is now, I am sure she sees them too, and that comforts my soul.

Somewhat against our better judgment, we took home a tiny tortoise-shell ginger, black and white kitten we called 'Maggie.' She was lively, intelligent and very clean. We were lucky in our choice. In no time at all she had Billie in his place—he kept a respectful distance from her. Then they became good friends, and inseparable. She spent most of her summer days in one of the cherry trees eying the birds without trying to catch them.

The previous owner was absolutely right when he said that each year both the Bing and the Queen Anne cherry trees produced bumper crops. I have no idea how many pounds we picked, but between both trees it must have been close to eighty. Gloria, whose natural talents ran in a quite different direction, was not an imaginative cook, but while she later became an excellent jam and marmalade maker, I made deep cherry pies by the dozen. We bought a fruit dryer and tried to dry, not only the cherries, but Armenian cucumbers, peaches and strawberries. One afternoon while browsing through a bookstore, we found a magazine on "How to dry Fruit." We thought that you simply put whatever it was into a dry, ventilated container and after a while dried fruit would appear—like in the store. Our ignorance provided hours of entertainment and fun. Never really serious about cooking, except at Christmas time and other festive occasions when we had guests, Gloria ran the kitchen with untutored culinary skills picked up at odd times during her non-stop life.

I could see Gloria's energy beginning to flag, especially noticeable in the morning when she got into her car to drive to Willows or Orland, each an hour's drive away, and I understood why. Red Bluff had nothing to offer her that would satisfy her need to rise to the top ranks of her profession. She wanted more contacts, especially of her equals in her profession and a wider field to satisfy her appetite to learn. She had started her counseling days in the drug treatment field, but I believe she wanted to get experience in more diversified form of mental illness.

For my own part, I learned very quickly that I (we) were not members of the Red Bluff cult. By that I mean we were easily recognizable as out of towner's by our dress and by the way we spoke, especially me (pure English). We were invited to go bowling but declined—it was not our pastime. I also noticed that nearly every male who wore jeans carried a tin of *skoal* chewing tobacco in his right hand back pocket. The imprint was clearly visible from a hundred yards. Casual conversation in the local coffee shop was stilted. It was time to move on.

*

A double tragedy struck us early in 1993. Both Billie and Maggie had really become part of the family. Part of our evening comfort in front of a blazing log fire, was to watch them both wind down and finally curl up with each other at one side of the grate.

Wilder Road, upon which we lived, had seen a huge increase in heavy traffic during the past few months. An "environmentalist" had set up a "soil aeration dump" at the north end of our street. Trucks laden with contaminated earth from gasoline pump sites, traveled from far and wide and dumped their cargo in this allotted space. We were assured by the contractor that almost all of the contaminant would disperse into the air and virtually nothing would be absorbed into the ground. We were concerned about our wells from which our only source of drinking water came. There were no complaints about contaminated well water, but all those living on the north end of our street complained about the increase in heavy traffic. We had been assured that four or five trucks would be the norm per day. One day I counted thirty-seven. One of them killed our Maggie. As I turned onto our street, I saw a little bundle of fur on the crown of the road a few yards from our house. There was little doubt in my mind that she had been struck by a heavy motor vehicle.

Billie's death a couple of months later was more personal. Our rose garden looked like rubbish; the buds were falling apart before they bloomed. I am no gardener but I was pretty sure that fish emulsion would help a lot. A local salvage shop had several five-gallon drums of concentrated fish meal. Imagining myself to be the head gardener at Kew Gardens, I spread this foul smelling mulch into the earth around the bushes.

Half an hour later, I heard Billie throwing up and rushed outside to find him by the rose beds, his muzzle daubed with the whitish fertilizer I had just dug into the soil, and blood coming out of his mouth. I grabbed the container and managed to see one word on the rusty label,'Chlorine' and two others ending in '. . . ine.' That was enough. I called the vet and told him what had happened. He asked me if I had an emetic; I said I didn't, so wrapped poor Billie in a plastic bag and drove him down town to the vet. I stayed there for a couple of hours while an emetic was administered, then watched as the vet put an IV into Billie's leg. All to no avail; he died overnight. The vet told me he'd also given him a pain killer. I hope that it was a narcotic and the poor guy didn't suffer very long. I blamed myself for not having read the label on the can more carefully, but in all fairness the label was travel worn, rusty and almost illegible, and it was sold as 'fishmeal.'

Poor Gloria was grief stricken and spent the following day wandering around the garden spending moments at both their graves, Maggie's, under the apple tree and Billie's in the back lot under a stone cairn. I carved, from an oak barrel stave, suitable headboards for each of our beloved friends.

Now it truly was time to go.

* * *

Chapter XII

We find a new Home

We had made a few friends in Red Bluff, particularly Phyllis and Wesley, our neighbors to the north. They were the ones who had told us about the abundance of spring flowers in Jones Valley, to our south, a shallow valley between the Pacific mountain range and the low foothills that stretched away south toward Red Bank, Black Butte and Williams. Each of both Spring seasons we spent on Wilder Road. We packed up a day's food and drink, usually in late May or early June, and slowly drove down unpaved Rte.162, stopping frequently to admire and photograph masses of California Poppies, blue and white Lupines, occasional hosts of Daffodils bobbing and nodding in the gentle breezes; an unending panorama of color accompanied by an almost indescribable, pervasive fragrance from flowers which have no individual distinguishing fragrance. Cattle and horses must have been in their element, grazing off a carpet of tiny yellow and red ground cover; Tom Thumb and Scarlet Pimpernel, that unrolled indolently toward the granite bluffs where eagles and hawks lived in small caves and on rock ledges well marked with bird-lime.

Included among our close friends were our two real estate agents with who guided us through the pitfalls of unintelligible escrow forms: Cherry Poulton and JoAnn Perkins. We relied on their judgment and their unwavering professional attention; we trusted them implicitly, and on several occasions had lunch or dinner with them.

Gloria had recently been obliged to leave a Post Office rental space she had taken during her first month in Red Bluff, and had found temporary office space in what used to be a small beauty parlor. She didn't like it very much, but. I believe that while she was on her own in Tehema and Glenn Counties, she felt like a pioneer woman, loving the challenge.

*

We had a discussion about our pulling out of Red Bluff, but there wasn't much to discuss. We therefore put our dinky little house on the market and contacted a large real estate agency in Redding. We spent a weekend touring the lots and inspecting many houses, some of which were sort-of okay, others out of the question. We had also spoken to one of the older, more senior agents in the agency, and explained as best we could, just what kind of a house we wanted.

On the following day we were at home wondering what to do about our Redding dilemma, when the phone rang. Our new found friend in the agency was at the other end excitedly telling us she had found "our House." And so it was. She had found a two story house at the eastern end of a quiet street and neighborhood: trees everywhere; a large garden with fruit trees, and views of both Mount Lassen and Mount Shasta, all we could ever wish for. Once again we had been blessed with an untiring agent who looked after our needs and wants.

Before we moved, we agreed to replace Billie. At the local pound the choices were limited, but in one kennel we found five black and white pups about eight weeks old. They were all scrapping around having a good time except one who was trying to sleep—he was on the bottom—and he was the one who became our Charlie, a Border Collie/Springer mix with the merest stub of a tail, obviously a cutting error on the part of whoever shortened his tail. Charlie became part of the family right away, endearing himself to us in so many ways. We would take him around the same field that Billie loved so much, and when he arrived back at the house the first thing he always did was cool his feet by placing all four of them in his drinking bowl. We could almost hear him say "Ah-h-h." He took to Gloria immediately, but took his time getting to know me.

The next four legged animal to join the family was Taz, a brindle colored calico cat found in the foundations of an office block on Oregon Street, Redding, where Gloria worked; one of a litter of five, and without doubt the fiercest of the bunch. She, however, didn't join our family until we moved to Redding. Even though Charlie was an 'old timer' so to speak, he soon found out where his place in the family was, and so did I—as far from Taz as possible. Gloria and she, however, were the best of friends. Taz was omnipresent; under your feet, in your face, next in line for food, and on Gloria's chest all night, every night. Taz's redeeming feature, if you are inclined to view her predator's skill as a virtue, was rat and mole catching; several in one night.

*

We moved to Woodhill Estates, east of Hilltop Drive, Redding, in May of 1993. The house was all that we ever dreamed of. There were three bedrooms; from the east-facing windows of one of them, one had a clear view of Mt. Lassen fifty miles away, and from the north facing window of another bedroom, the 14,500 ft. peak of Mt. Shasta, could be seen through a stand of cottonwood trees. Perhaps the best feature of our new house was the quietude. The only sound that broke the night silence was the occasional sad wail of a locomotive and the yipping of coyotes that lived in a nearby green belt.

In a city where there are many mental health professionals, Gloria started cautiously as counselor at a large Catholic Agency (NVCSS-Northern Valley Catholic Social Services) whose prime purpose is to provide social services to the common people at an affordable price—food, clothing, housing and mental health counseling. She worked happily there for about a year, but told me one day that the big drawback at NVCSS that she felt 'stuck.' She explained. Working for an agency that looks after the less wealthy has its disadvantages. Magnanimous as the agency was, their employees were not paid quite as much as they may have been paid elsewhere, particularly the counseling staff, who at that time, were not considered as necessary as they truly were. Gloria's only complaint was that the pay did not match her qualifications, RN, MFCC.(now MFT).

Seeking employment with another agency, she got the job but soon found that the only difference was a minute increase in pay.

She moved to yet another agency. Within months of working for this one she knew she had made another error in judgment, and immediately made plans to place her own shingle on her own front door.

One counselor, DaLene Forester, became Gloria's closest friend. They were alike in personality and were blessed with similar senses of humor. DaLene had passed her final exams, but had 3000 hours of internship to complete before she could be eligible to assume the title of MFT. All the therapists I know believe that to be successful counselor you had to have a good sense of humor.

After much discriminatory searching, Gloria and DaLene found a small unfurnished house on Court Street in Redding, for rent. Gloria agreed without hesitation, to oversee her new buddy during the internship. Each of them set up and furnished their own offices.

During this very busy time of moving and adjustment, I offered my services as general handyman. I painted whatever they wished and cleaned the office each week and performed odd jobs as they turned up. They paid me; I was very happy.

It was here that their bond of friendship became firm. They stayed at that house for two years and each built up a small clientele some of whom followed them. They spent quite a bit of off-time doing things together. They made trips to conferences and workshops together. They even invited me to accompany them on an E.M.D.R conference in Mexico, not far from Mazatlan. I enjoyed the holiday at a nice hotel overlooking the Pacific Ocean. I also enjoyed endless beaches where I was free every morning to ogle. I remember well the free time we all spent together on the terrace where the swimming pool was and hearing their laughter. It was a precious time.

During the winter months, Redding can get cold and wet and at some time both Gloria and DaLene decided that the rental house had too man faults, leaking roofs and window panes.

Without considering the end-cost, they went office-hunting and picked a pleasant, rather upscale office off Airpark Road, where they shared the rent for the office space. They spent about a year at that office, made good friends with two psychologists who had office space in the same building, but decided that however pleasant the new offices were, they were too small and too expensive.

Searching for other therapists who may have been looking for office space, they were fortunate to find three who gladly accepted their offer to join them in a five-office house on West Street.

Gloria was, at last in her element. Contented, surrounded by bright, similar-minded colleagues, and her friend, DaLene, she rapidly established her name as she investigated, and became skilful at some of the newer aspects of healing the mind.

*   *   *

Chapter XJJJ

Gloria unfolds

Gloria took a great chance when she married me. She knew much about my life shortly after we met, most importantly, that I was a recovering alcoholic who had been sober for a mere ten days or so when we first met. For those whose knowledge of alcoholism may be sparse, three excellent and simple adjectives that describe the disease of alcoholism are, *cunning, baffling and powerful*: *Once an alcoholic, always an alcoholic.* Remembering that at any time during our alcoholic lives, one drink is too many and a thousand is not enough, I had been sober for the third time in twenty years. I knew it and so did she.

She, knowing that rationalization is the alcoholic's way of finding a way out of difficulties, knew, just as I did, that we (alcoholics) carry around in our heads a permanent committee that meets each time we run into a problem.

Allow me to present a short vignette of a typical committee meeting:-

Com: *"Oh!Oh! I see you've got yourself into a spot of trouble."*
Me: *"What do you mean, 'it's nothing to worry about?"*
Com: *"Remember the last time you borrowed money, you went out and got drunk because you couldn't pay it back."*
Com: *"You don't have to get drunk, Peter. Why do you always think that?"*
Me *"No,no! You are probably quite right; just one little drink will get me thinking straight. Just one, eh? Makes me feel good already and takes away the problem."*

That is the sort of mind-game the alcoholic plays on himself—and during the first few years of sobriety, it often works.

And so we set off together hand in hand on a perilous road of uncertainty—and she knew exactly what the stakes were.

Because I had heard the phrase, "Keep coming Back" so many times from so many recovering drunks, I knew it was the right thing to do both for me and Gloria and I was not going to let her down. I went to AA two and three times a week. I got involved in AA. I worked on a part of myself that I had rarely thought about, my soul or my spirit. And I stayed sober without any interference from the addicted side of me. If I said, "Gloria made me do it," I would be paying tribute where it does not belong. Rather I might say, "I worked on my spirituality because Gloria was—Gloria."

I suffered from a mild depression most of my life. Why? A psychoanalyst would probably explain it by pointing out that I was a sensitive child who lost his father in a cruel sea accident too early in life, and had grown up longing for that which he may have missed—a man's influence. That may be true because I often thought about and sometimes dreamt of the last time I saw my dad—naked on the engine room floor plates taking a bath from a bucket. The incident occurred one evening in April, 1936 when my mother took me down to the docks to see my father off to sea. I was wandering around the ship and happened to look down into the steamy, oily depths below and saw a man, naked, bending over a bucket washing himself I withdrew hastily, because I was only ten, then cautiously peeked again; It was my dad. I was immediately consumed with a flood of emotions from guilt, to shame, to horror but mostly as though I had committed a mortal sin. That vision no longer haunts me. I can think of it and dismiss the memory in an instant without any recurrences.

One Sunday afternoon, Gloria asked me if I would like to work on 'my dad's memory.' I reluctantly agreed. She told me to get comfortable in my favorite chair, breathe easily and relax. She then sat on the arm of my chair, held my hand and began to talk in a voice quite new to me. There was a distinct clear timbre to it: slightly lower than I remembered, but with a palliative quality. She talked to me for a number of minutes as though I were a small boy. She asked me a few questions about my early life. She told me to completely relax, put both her hands on my forehead—and left. I dozed on for a few minutes and then woke up knowing that something was different but not what it was.

The following morning I figured out what had changed. I felt lighter of heart; in short, my dad had left me; I had let him go. I hugged Gloria and thanked her for a "miracle." I heard her say, "I'm happy for you: no miracle, just know-how."

*

Another example of Gloria's mastery of her talents and her caring nature occurred in 1991, when we were living in Lakewood. A young friend of mine who lived in England and whom I had not seen for many years, announced that she and her husband would be in southern California and could they visit us?

They arrived late one afternoon. Gloria and I were on the front lawn to receive them. I heard Gloria's murmur of alarm as my friend got out of the car. The cause of her alarm was soon apparent: my young friend seemed to be no more than bag of bones. She had assumed a bent posture, which turned out to be part of the disease, and her face, still a pretty one, had lost its contours; the skin was so tightly drawn over her cheek bones and jaw, that the outline of her skull and the capillary veins were clearly visible.

While they were in their room unpacking, Gloria pulled me into the kitchen and whispered, "She hasn't got very long to live: anorexia. I've never seen the disease so advanced."

Alarmed by what I had just heard, I hastily looked it up in our medical dictionary.

It didn't say much. *Anxiety, eating disorder, desire to be thin . . .* and a few more fragmentary remarks on the general body deterioration. I wondered how on earth a simple desire to be thin, could cause a person to lose his/her life? I discovered later that it was much more complicated that that.

Her husband was not affected, at least not outwardly, although I am sure that he must inwardly, have been distressed, being conscious of his wife's condition. She ate sparingly of some salad for dinner, and that was that. After they had gone to bed, Gloria confirmed my doubts about the simplicity with which Anorexia had been described in the medical book, and enlarged on many more psychological causes. "She needs an extensive course in therapeutic recovery," was about the extent of my understanding.

The following day Gloria and my friend went out shopping, during the course of which Gloria told her that her body was slowly shutting down, and that it was only a matter of time, unless drastic changes were undertaken, before she would die. They became fast friends. They left for London a day or so later. Tears were shed at the airport: real displays of grief and concern.

Upon arrival in their hometown, my young friend immediately sought a recovery center, signed up and started a long course of treatment. Both Gloria and I were in almost daily contact with her by way of email and telephone. Her recovery was difficult and lengthy. Each day we talked to her, Gloria passed on her wisdom, advising her that her disease was so much like alcoholism that the treatment would follow the A.A principles of Twelve Steps. While I encouraged her with highlights from my own recovery from Alcoholism, one of our maxims being, *"One Day at a Time"* . . . *live for the moment you are in, remember just today. Do not think of tomorrow for it is not yet part of your life, and may never be."* In short, *"LET GO:LET GOD."* Gloria dealt with the onset of the disease, which she quickly concluded was our friends' loss of her father to Altzheimer's a few years back. It seems that she had been singularly devoted to her father, perhaps relying solely on him for guidance; whereas the relationship with her mother was not that good. Seemingly there had been a lot of filial criticism from her mother, and it was in this area of mental health that Gloria showed her expertise.

Several years later we visited them at their home. My friend had not put on a great deal of weight, but her face glowed with health and happiness. She still ate sparsely and does so to this day. Her life, however, has been restored—and we are inseparable friends.

*

Shortly after we moved to Redding, Gloria heard about, and subsequently read about, Energy Psychology. This new approach to understanding our emotions and steering them into a place where they could be directed to work for us instead of against us, appealed greatly to Gloria. It was a great step toward her own elementary beliefs that our bodies were not simply large sacks of flesh containing the organic machinery that kept us alive and breathing, but that our hearts and brains were themselves vibrant organs that strove, seemingly of their own volition, to regulate our lives: harness the energy produced and direct it into a healing process.

Candace Pert PhD, Research Professor at Georgetown University, in her foreword to the book, *The Promise of Energy Psychology,* writes of the book itself, "... *is a synthesis of practices designed to deliberately shift the molecules of emotion. These practices have three distinct advantages over psychiatric medicines. They are non-invasive, highly specific, and have no side-effects. Energy interventions impact the body's intricate electrochemical system as well as more subtle energies. Subtle Energy is a term born of an emerging paradigm that is still just outside the embrace of western science, though it has long been central to the worldview of Eastern medicine and spiritual disciplines.*"

Ms. Pert has, I think, professionalized my layman's explanation.

In what I might call *a recent surge in the psychological treatment of human ailments,*

Albert Schoppenhauer, a nineteenth century German philosopher wrote:

All Truth goes through three stages. "First, it is ridiculed.

Second: Then it is violently opposed.

And Finally, it is accepted as self-evident."

I mention these conclusions because I went through this complete phase when Gloria announced that she was about to start her course on Energy Psychology and would be spending one week at Otter Point on the Oregon coast under the tutelage of Donna Eden and Gary Craig.

She came back full of enthusiasm and a great deal of practical knowledge about the connection between our emotions and our brains. Briefly, the connection is an electrochemical one, and what makes the link to the brain is the tapping on certain electrochemical circuits at various places on our bodies, wrists, forehead, side of the head and upper part of the chest. The therapist asks the client certain questions related to the particular fear or mental condition that is distressing the client, and is then directed to think of some suitable, peaceful thought and at the same time tap him or herself on the circuit points in a directed sequence. After one or several procedures, the client will admit to feeling less of the unwanted emotion, and most often will concede that the dreaded feeling has left him/her.

I have tried to demonstrate above, the bare outlines of a non-invasive procedure that works. There is so much more to the theory and practice, but the basic outlines show that the antidote is simple and self-administered. *(read "The Promise of Energy Psychology" by David Feinstein, Donna Eden and Gary Craig")* I pooh-poohed the idea right away; then gave Gloria a hard time each time I saw her practicing it, and finally gave in and tried it myself.

The next non-invasive therapeutic process, about which Gloria became excited, was the Eye Movement Desensitization & Reprocessing theory (EMDR developed by Francine Shapiro PhD, Senior Research Fellow at the Mental Research Institute, Palo Alto, California.

Gloria, always seeking a holistic approach to emotional problems, immediately saw the intrinsic value of EMDR and commenced a course of training, level I, in July of 1994. Under the tutelage of the founder herself, Francine Shapiro, she complete level II in August of 1995. Again, in February 1999, we both traveled to a small coastal village in Mexico named Tomatalan a few miles north of Manzanillo, where, Francine Shapiro PhD and Robert Tinker PhD, gave a week-long conference on the values and practices of EMDR. With her profound capability of absorbing pertinent data, Gloria moved on with Advanced Clinical Applications of EMDR and was finally deemed proficient in the technique of working with those whom she thought would benefit from the therapy of that art. Thereafter, with her friend and colleague, DaLene Forester, she attended international association conferences in many parts of the United States and Canada.

Gloria possessed an unquenchable thirst for expanding her skills, gaining knowledge in the field of psychotherapy. Not a conference or lecture that afforded her CEU's, went unattended. Without being a perfectionist, she became a fervent believer in the importance of the legal and ethical side of being a psychotherapist and developed a meticulousness about *"dotting her I's and crossing her T's.*

In 1998, the Board of Behavioral Health in Sacramento was recruiting MFT's (Marriage and Family Therapists) to learn the tricky business of becoming Oral Examiners for those interns whom, having completed the requisite number of hours under supervision, wished to take the examination at M.A level, which would get them a license to practice psychotherapy. Gloria applied, took the training and spent time both in Sacramento and Marin County examining candidates.

Remembering her own experience in 1985, when she took the exam, she was not too keen on the task. She said, however, after her examining days were over, that it was an invaluable part of her own education.

In the year 2000, a small university, National University in Redding, had upgraded its level of advanced education from B.A in various subjects to M.A in Counseling Psychology, and was looking for teachers. Gloria applied and was taken on. This, for her, was another adventure into a world where she was dealing with people who needed help (knowledge), but some of whom were afflicted with narcissism, and instead of learning would often try to *teach*. All of Gloria's training during her last thirty-five years now had to focus on her own reactions to some hostility to which she was not accustomed.

She dealt with the situations in her own manner—quietly and without resentment, and with her own brand of humor. She taught from 2000 until 2003.

Going through her résumé, I was astonished at the depth of her professional education, the number of organizations to which she had become affiliated and the faculties at which she had taught. She had lectured on Cross Cultural Counseling at La Verne University, a Board Member of Kid's Turn, Redding, a facilitator for the Nurse Diversion Support Group, the American Red Cross Disaster Mental Health Group to name a few.

*

I used to think that Gloria's spiritual life was much the same as mine, lukewarm, perhaps tepid and vague. She had been brought up in a religious vise manufactured bytheBaptists' beliefs in the precise and literal wording of the Bible, which in my own opinion is a lengthy, partial-fiction history of our creation. Occasionally we would get into a, *"that's nothing, Wait till I tell you about the Catholic (Baptist) . . ."* It was never a

Discussion, but rather a litany of undignified incursions we had each suffered under the disguise of religious guidance.

I had spent most of my religious learning under the guidance of the Dominican Monks, a very liberal, philosophical order. Even though our instruction was very thorough, it was not Bible based. I do believe that the Dominicans had a different concept of a Divine Being in the realm of the hereafter. When I left school in 1943, age seventeen, and was catapulted into a world into in which the lifestyle and the language was completely foreign to me, it didn't take long for me to absorb the ships' atmosphere without interference of religious effect. I soon forgot about God and His so-called mercies and found out very rapidly that I'd better look after myself if I wanted to stay alive. After four years of grueling, often dangerous work, the once constant awareness of the Divine Architect had dwindled to periodic penetrating memories of the Dominicans and the accompanying stabs of guilt. Later in life, I stranded myself on the lonely reef of alcoholism. Twenty years later, I rescued myself from that solitary confinement and thanked my Higher Power for the miracle. But I was never quite sure that it was 'my' Higher Power or 'a' Higher Power to whom I had to offer thanks.

Gloria on the other hand, became steeped in the Baptist faith both from the church she attended every Sunday, and her parents who, with watchful eye, saw sinful worldliness besiege her youthful hormones and her eagerness to be 'normal' without apparent effect. She was a good girl! After she graduated and became a student nurse, she too joined this strange world where everything she had been taught was naughty, was in fact, practiced by everyone. She and a group of student nurses, spent a couple of weeks on board a yacht in the Bahamas with an Australian rugby football team. Although she seldom spoke about her early adventures, that one must have been a *Baptist Bible Breaker.*

As she grew older and worldly acumen displaced or diluted her biblical teachings, I believe she did not dismiss many of the questions she had about God, heaven and hell and the hereafter, but set them aside in that boundless mind of hers to be examined later.

This she did during the last year of her life on earth.

*

Gloria, in her search for professional fulfillment had, I metaphorically thought, left me behind to look after the house and to perform all things pertaining to housekeeping. But each day she worked in Redding, she left at 07:15 and returned at 7.00pm unless something interfered. Like a marine superintendent watching the departure of his commodore ship, I would stand at the door, kiss her, ask her to drive carefully and wave to her just before she rounded the turn at the end of the street. In the evening

I would watch for her car to pull up and greet her as though she'd been on a transatlantic voyage. There was no mistaking the contentment on her face as she came through the front door. The flowers from our garden during the summer months filled vases in every room we used regularly, and from Half Moon Bay or from Honduras, in winter. Gloria had a curious mind, and from time to time she would embark on a reading spree on whatever subject was at the surface of her mind. Hopi Indian spiritual practices. She once attempted to read the St. James version of the Bible, but somewhere between covers she shrugged her shoulders and said, "I don't really feel encouraged by anything I have read in this book." She read everything there was on Energy Medicine. The brain, however, was her greatest source of interest. She watched PBS's 'Nova' and every documentary on the brain. One of her hero's was Dr. Daniel Amen PhD.

Whereas I was a 'fair weather' gardener, Gloria loved to kneel in all weathers and pull weeds. On free weekends we spent many hours reading and drinking Blackberry-Sage Tea under a huge white oak and a fruited mulberry in the garden. Nothing could give me more pleasure than to see her stretched out on the *chaise longue* getting some rays. She loved pansies, not only because they lasted a long time, but because they were a border flower and easy to plant. However, many of our weekends were shattered. There were conferences to go to, workshops to attend, and once in a while, clients to see. But we made up for these infrequent interruptions by taking a cruise to Alaska, in 2004 on the *Veendam*, by my standards, a large comfortable ship with a well-trained crew and excellent cooks.

Our pre-voyage instructions from Holland America Line were to fly to Anchorage then take a company-provided bus to Seward on the Kenai Peninsula, where *Veendam* lay alongside; about ninety miles south of the main airport. It was September when we arrived in Alaska, and cold. My visions of a peaceful cruise began to vanish. We stayed overnight in a hotel and shivering, found our way to the bus the following morning. Faced with a four-hour road trip, our spirits rose slightly when we discovered that the bus was the latest in buses. Almost as soon as we got under-way, our young bus driver announced that he would cheer us up by reciting, not some, but all of the poetic works of Robert Service. He strummed a bar or two on a guitar—and began. Two hours later we had passed our point of no return and Zeb, our reader, had just embarked on another batch of poems about the life of Dan McGrew. Gloria, I could tell, was not familiar with the works of Service and often punched me in the ribs and asked me what he was saying or what a certain word meant. Her heartfelt delight showed all over her face, and mine, as we pulled up alongside the cruise ship. The entire busload of future passengers left the vehicle with smiles on their faces, having just listened to the Cremation of Dan McGee.

I viewed *Veendam* from a distance with the jaundiced eye of an ancient mariner. Not a pretty ship: The old words that described the ships I'd sailed on contained words like, *sheer lines, camber forecastle Head and poop-deck.* None of these fitted. The closest I got to any kind of description of this maritime apology, was large oblong steel box filled with cabins and people. To the modern-day sailor, that description might be cruel.

Our assigned cabin was #832, a very comfortable room, square in shape situated on the centerline, almost amidships and about thirty feet below the main deck level. Gloria showed some concern at our cabins' position in the ship.

"Herr Peter, we are so far down. What happens if we have a collision—or something?" I tried to explain to her that our cabin was in fact at about the ships'tipping center, technically known as the Metacenter—that spot in a ship which theoretically remains in the same place in regard to the rest of the ships' movement i.e pitching or rolling.

"Easy for you to say," she smartly replied, "but what happens to the meta—whatever, when we have a collision?"

"We won't have a collision," I replied in a sort of bored-superior tone, "ships don't collide these days." And left it at that.

The weather in Seward, when we departed, was not promising. The ships' weather station forecast some rough seas and gale force winds (up to seventy knots). With the knowledge that we were on board a fifty-six thousand ton cruise liner, we ended our busy evening early and went to bed. Not a movement from this huge ship. Gloria hung on my arm as we got out of the elevator on 'F' deck, our deck.

"You are right, Herr Peter," she said, "not a movement." That is, until 3:am when we were both rudely awakened by (I guessed) a rather larger, steeper wave curled under the flair of the starboard bow and brought *Veendam* to a frame shuddering stop. The impact activated all the emergency sensors in the engine room including the main breaker, which disconnected and threw the ship into darkness.

Gloria literally hurled herself at me, yelling, "What happened, are we going to be alright?

"Absolutely," I replied, as though nothing much had happened, yet feeling her shake in my arms "we've been socked by a big wave; the lights will be on in a minute or two." And like magic, they came on. We talked about the incident for a few minutes. She slowly calmed down. Glasses of water we had placed by our bunks had not spilled or even shifted.

Breakfast that morning was, perhaps, the most interesting meal of the voyage. We learned that two older passengers had suffered heart attacks. The 'self-serve' lounge was only half full; most of the passengers there did not appear to be enjoying the sumptuous repast. Gloria, contrary to her oft-repeated excuses for declining water trips, was not sea-sick, and enjoyed a hearty breakfast.

We tried to walk outside on the promenade deck, but the weather made it dangerous. The ship would often lurch causing the unwary to stumble. We went inside and spent some time in the Library. The call at Sitka, a tricky place to get into, was cancelled because of the poor weather conditions. Valdez, where the Exxon Valdez ran aground on an offshore reef in March 1989 and spilled her entire cargo of crude oil, millions of gallons, most of which end up on the shoreline, was included as a port of call.

We docked at Valdez during the evening and landed the two patients with heart trouble. The following day we took a couple of tours of the city. First we were herded into a small theater where we watched fourteen robust, but handsome, Russian women perform traditional dances of the Ukraine and Georgia. Dressed in colorful blouses and jackets and long skirts from under which one could see polished boots, they received much appreciative applause. Someone even threw a bouquet onto the stage The dancers did their best to look as though they enjoyed themselves, but since a cruise ship arrived here every day, and they were obliged to dance every day, I can imagine they looked forward to an Alaskan winter.

While at Valdez, I took particular notice of as much of the shoreline as I could see. I was surprised to see little or no signs of the massive oil spill. Of course it had been eleven years ago, but even so, the cleanliness of the port and facilities struck me as nothing more than, astonishing. I could only conclude that the cleanup crews supplied by Exxon had done a magnificent job. I remember following the Court of Enquiry and the condemnation of the Master of the ship on whose shoulders the Coast Guard placed the entire blame. The findings made me cross. I think that the blame should have been apportioned.

During the afternoon and early evening, we took a tour of the Denali Federal Reserve, which included a visit to the Bald Eagle infirmary where injured Bald Eagles are sought and brought to the dispensary. Most of the injuries sustained are to the wing bones and legs, usually caused by contact with electric overhead wires. Nearly all the birds treated require a protracted period of partial immobility. Suitably attired lab technicians splint and/or tape the injured limb and secure the animals to a tree stump in a wired-off enclosure where they can readily be observed at all times. When a bird is thought fit to resume its wild life, the medical staff hold a small ceremony, which they hope will encourage the animal to return to this haven in the wilds of Alaska, where pure love and dedication drives these young veterinarians to attend the needs of these wounded eagles.

We were also invited to view a handler displaying his skills when at close quarters with these fierce birds. One of the daunting jobs of the handlers was to transport it manually from building to building in the facility.

The handler brought the bird into the exhibition room on his hand with the bird's talons firmly encasing the gauntleted thumb and hand of the carrier. The bird apparently knew his handler, for when he shifted the bird to his shoulder, it began to nuzzle his head and preen his hair. This brought loud applause from the watching crowd. Seemingly in response to the approbation, the animal plucked a large clump of the handler's hair out of his scalp, at which point he decided to end the show.

We learned that these birds of prey mate for life; the female lays three of four eggs of which the pair share the incubation. We were surprised to hear that along with its usual prey of rabbits and foxes, Golden Eagles in particular have been known to fly off with mountain goats, and on one occasion, a suckling colt from the mare's side.

Before we left the forest, we were given a grand tour of the reservation, which included the site for recovering birds. There they sat, tethered to a stump, twenty feet off the ground, staring with that inimitable ferocity into the middle distance waiting with the patience of the succored.

Gloria, if only by the expression on her face, was obviously enthralled by the experience. With an ear-to-ear smile she whispered to me, "Now that's the kind of job mine is, but with human emotions."

The weather had calmed to slights seas and swells when we at last stopped a Juneau, the capitol city of Alaska. We had booked a whale-watching trip with some doubts, for whales sometimes become scarce, especially when boatloads of people are tight up there on the surface of their domain.

For the first four hours, we did not sight a hump back whale but many Orca's, which seemed impervious to the noises of motor boats. Finally we had several displays of hump backs on a feeding spree. The skipper told us how they capture small fish. The first sign that something is about to happen is when flocks of seagulls hover in flocks just above the water. Soon a couple of whales surfaced and slapped their tails on the surface. Pretty soon we could see that six or seven whales had collected all nose to nose. Then they sank below the surface, and this, the skipper told us, is how they "bubble-net," entrap herring or small, similar fish. They isolate a large shoal of small fish by surrounding it then blowing bubbles. This confuses the prey and they swim round and round. Meanwhile, the whales slowly rise to the surface, still blowing bubbles and trapping the small fish within a cylinder of bubbles. At the right time, each whale opens his maw wide; captive fish simply fall, unobstructed into the gaping jaws together with a vast amount of seawater. The excess water is blown through each whales blowhole—and the fish sustain the whales' appetite for an hour.

The packet boat skippers were courteous and patient, and allowed up to witness a few more "bubble nettings."

*

A visit to Glacier Bay caused many of us some awed sadness. The big glaciers, indeed all of them, are receding due to 'global warming' if, indeed, that is the real cause of the recess. Nonetheless, they are not where they were ten years ago. Reading the statistics, I had a fantasy that they would disappear before our eyes. The Mendenhall

Glacier, the broadest, has receded two hundred feet in three hundred and sixty days. There are 6,080 feet in a nautical mile. It will be around the year 2040 before the leading edge of the glacier has receded thirty miles. Glaciers are simply trillions of tons of compressed snow/ice. I was interested in the blue ice one could see close to the waters edge where the compressed carbon could clearly be seen. Gloria, although impressed by the enormity and ages of these ice rivers, would only comment that they were frigid and lifeless.

We disembarked at Vancouver, B.C. early Saturday morning where an old shipmate of mine picked us up. We spent a delightful weekend in their North Vancouver home. We took the ferry to Vancouver on Sunday, and were home in bed by 10:pm. still reminiscing about our magical voyage.

*   *   *

Chapter XIV

The Disease

The first wisp of cloud that heralded the future storm and terrible tragedy that lay ahead, for Gloria and me, came in early May 2005. Gloria told me somewhat nervously that she had noticed a trace of blood in the toilet bowl. She added that she thought the cause was probably hemorrhoids, which had bothered her off and on for some time. Gloria had always been fit and healthy and I gave the news little attention.

A week later when she arrived home from work, rather later in the evening than usual, I could see that she wasn't her usual smiling self. I gave her a "what's up" look. She, almost tremulously, took hold of my arm and said, "Peter, I think I have cancer."

For a moment I couldn't think, let alone give her any kind of answer.

"*CANCER?*" It came out hoarsely, as though I had lost breath. "How do you know sweetheart"? I led her over to the sofa and we sat down. She looked at me with an expression I had never seen on her face before

"After I told you about the bleeding," she said in a low voice "I went to see Dr. Smith (her gynecologist). She took a sample and recommended that I get an MRI, just to be sure." She paused for a few seconds as though gathering her resources "Well the results came back today." She handed me a technical photograph and said, "This is a picture of my cancer."

I glanced at a grainy photograph, which left no doubt in my mind what it depicted.

Gloria, having told the worst, went on, "It's a 1cm x 1cm wart right at the anal sphincter. "The doctor has taken a biopsy. The results will be back on Monday."

"So you don't really know whether you have cancer or not." She looked at me, her eyes brimming.

"Not really," she said hesitantly, the tears now pouring down her face. "But suppose it is? What will we do?" I knew nothing about cancer; neither did Gloria. We sat together for at least two hours talking about the bare elements of what we knew of the disease. Gloria could only remember, from her nursing days, that most people with cancer died.

Sleep that night was out of the question. We both tossed and turned. The following morning, after a cup of coffee, we mutually agreed to make the best of a sunny weekend. And try not to dwell on Monday's verdict. We visited some of Gloria's old NVCSS buddies who kept us busy with tid-bits from the old establishment.

By Monday morning we both had attained some sort of composure, but the fear lurked just below the surface.

I accompanied Gloria down to the Imaging Clinic. We didn't have long to wait. A very pleasant doctor, the one who had first seen the image, told us that the biopsy was positive for cancer. He put his arm around Gloria's shoulders, and while we walked toward the entry told her not to overly worry because this small tumor was new, and the oncologists, he thought, would take care of it quickly. I must say, for my part, those words were like music to my ears. My attempts at cheering Gloria up were partially successful. She did smile once or twice, but I knew where her mind was.

We went to the oncology Department at Mercy shortly afterwards and saw both the Radiologist and the Oncologist. Gloria now appeared to be composed. I suppose I was too, until I thought the tone of voice the 'experts' used was a little flippant. Were Gloria coming for a tonsillectomy, it may have been appropriate: but cancer; one of the deadliest diseases in the world? In short, however, what they advised us was that chemotherapy and radiation given in regulated doses would soon have this small, apparently recently formed tumor, whipped. I became quite angry at their smiling faces, and in retrospect think that the prediction was both callow and cruel. As it turned out, that fresh tumor metamorphosed into a deadly, scavenging squamous cell carcinoma, which, five years later, grew and took possession of the lining of her pelvis—and killed her.

Not only was she facing the incursion of a cancer, she was also facing the only three known cures and arresting agents—*excision, chemotherapy and radiation* the former of which has limited practical latitude, the second a deadly mixture of chemicals given (usually) intravenously and intended to deprive the cancer of all blood supplies, and finally radiation, x-rays, supposedly directed with pin-point accuracy at the tumor site intended to burn and eradicate all that the chemicals had failed to accomplish.

Without drawing on the vast worldwide library of documents listing failures in the treatment of cancer in all its forms, I shall record as accurately as possible, the various and sometimes muddled attempts to rid my wife of cancer.

After huge doses of 5FU chemical, all apparently per protocol, accompanied by regulated shots of radiation over a period of three weeks, Gloria became ill; vomiting, diarrhea and loss of strength and weight. How the doctors missed her blood analysis, which I'm sure they took every day, I don't know, but it became obvious to me that she was declining fast. I finally yelled and complained enough to capture the attention of a woman doctor who immediately arranged for Gloria to be taken to the Intensive Care Unit. The first test taken there, showed that her blood supply had become septic; she had septicemia.

I cannot say enough in praise of the ICU doctor who knew enough to realize that Gloria was not far from death. I was allowed into the ICU whenever I could, and watched this doctor perform his miracle. He explained every medical tube that went down her throat or nose and every x-ray taken. After ten days of intensive care, he told me that she was going to be all right. I stayed at the hospital all night, and the following day Gloria knew who I was.

A couple of days later, she was moved to the oncology ward where a wonderful team of oncology nurses brought her back to health. I brought her home in late July 2005.

It was a much quieter; more serious and pensive Gloria that now lived with me. For a few days we just sat in the garden and talked over some of the incidents that had frightened her during her month-long stay at Mercy. Still frail and missing most of her hair, which didn't bother her very much: "It'll grow back soon enough." She often reminded me, she and I took walks on the newly opened Sundial Bridge. The River and the general ambience of the area soon put some color in her cheeks and strengthened her legs.

She underwent another MRI; this one showed a crater where the tumor once had been.

Gloria was thrilled. "It's gone, it's gone," she yelled about every hour. Further tests, however, revealed an indicator that a few cancer cells were probably lingering somewhere in her lower abdomen.

She went back to work after a couple of weeks' recuperation, telling me not to fuss: "I have clients waiting for me, and their need is greater than mine." During the months of autumn, she had two or three episodes of urinary tract infections. She was admitted to Mercy for the most severe, but the others she stayed at home and took an anti-biotic. She hardly missed a day at her office.

Mercy oncologist asked her to return for more treatment in order to get rid of what cancer cells remained. The memories of her last admission, particularly the infusion of the chemical that nearly killed her, made her shy away and finally decide not to return to the mercies of oncologists she didn't trust, but to take another course.

About this time, a minute, 1.mm fistula made itself manifest between her legs directly below her pelvis through the dermal wall. Even though fluid found its way through the aperture, Gloria, knowing that it was further evidence of cancer, padded up and continued work. However a well known OBGYN Surgeon practicing in Contra Costa County was recommended by a good friend, and we decided to visit him.

The trip to Walnut Creek in Contra Costa is long and tortuous. We got to his clinic at about 2:pm. He was a tall, rather severe looking individual, but also a no-nonsense man. I was allowed to be in the clinic during the examination. I watched him use a speculum to examine Gloria's lower interior. He took his time over it, jotting notes on a pad, and using extra light to get a better perspective. Twenty minutes later he told Gloria he had seen enough, and presumably knew enough from her reports from Mercy to make recommendations.

He did not minimize the extent of cancer but told us that in order to retard the further invasion of the cancer he knew of and could detect, he would have to remove her bladder and bowel and all of the female organs and nodes. The technical name for this type of surgery is *Pelvic Exenteration.*

I watched Gloria's face pale and flinch, but there was no hesitation I her voice when she asked him if he could leave her bladder, he replied." I'm afraid not, Mrs. Wright. If I operate on you, I will remove every expendable organ that may contain cancer cells."

"May I call you later to give you my decision?" she said in a small voice: so unlike Gloria.

The doctor looked in his appointments book and told us that he was being appointed to another university hospital in another state in two weeks, but if it was agreeable to her he would appoint another surgeon, a student of his, whom he highly recommended, to perform the operation. Without any hesitation, Gloria declined and said that she would seek a further opinion.

A friend of who lived nearby had heard of Gloria's troubles and came around to see her. After a few hours of discussion, Gloria's spirits had risen tremendously. She almost excitedly told me, after her friend had gone, that a doctor at Stanford Medical Center had performed a partial removal of her friends' internal organs for a condition similar in nature to that of Gloria, but had not removed her bladder. "He's my man." She announced with what might be described as relief.

Stanford Medical Clinic made an appointment for her to see the renowned oncology gynecologist two or three months hence.

Meanwhile Gloria, ever mindful of her clients, returned to work. I believe that the period between the first *Obgyn* surgery and the second (the last), a year later, was when she used her talents and her personal charisma to perform her best work.

Gloria never discussed her work with me. Her work was confidential. Once in a while she would come home brimming with joy, and she would tell me that she had had a difficult case but had, that day, found a solution to her client's problem. During her last year, 2008, during which she practiced her profession for about nine months, she expressed joy and pleasure such as I have described, several times. Her face would light up, such as I have never seen before.

After the second Ceremony of Gloria's life, (after her death), in which the entire mental health community of Redding enjoined, I had the chance to talk to several couples and some singles, whose lives, they claimed, Gloria had changed. There were some whose children's future's were in jeopardy because of some legal injunction, and which

Gloria's wit and perspicacity had reasoned, overcome and been received well in court. There were others whose problems were personal, and who simply approached me and told me that they loved Gloria and could not have survived without her loving counsel.

*   *   *

Chapter XV

The Last Battle

The once 1mm fistula, grew larger each day. When we applied for entry into Stanford Hospital and the services of a certain well known surgeon, it had widened to 1.cm and the fluid discharge, dark and foul smelling. Our first encounter with her surgeon was positive. A Very gentle and caring man, but careful too. The examination took less than an hour. He was of the opinion that the fistula would eventually heal itself. The examination itself covered only the parts visible by speculum and intense light; the full extent could only be seen during the upcoming operation. Then we drove 250 miles back to Redding. We made five such visits, each from and back to Redding, before the surgeon announced a date for surgery. He said it would take ten hours for him to excise all that was necessary, he would however, not touch the bladder. Gloria was thrilled. Because of the length of surgery, he went on, would she kindly have the colostomy done at Mercy in Redding, because he could then be free to perform his job without the risk of contamination.

The idea of having a colostomy certainly did not thrill Gloria, but she faced it stoically and named herself "the bag lady" long before the surgery.

The surgery, performed during the latter part of 2007, went well. The purpose of the operation was to create a false anus by cutting the lower part of the colon and directing the end of the colon through the hole the surgeon had just provided in the patient's side: a medically approved almost-water tight bag is then set in place: waste matter then falls into the bag and is removed and emptied as often as necessary. You can imagine that during the course of a year, one can get through as many as 1000 bags-very expensive—very tiresome.

Equipped with her bag (s) and a dauntless smile but always dressed beautifully, Gloria left the house each morning to attend to the needs of her clients. Once in a while, I would get a call from her during the day asking me to 'bring down a couple of 'bags'. After seeing her under those conditions and marveling at her courage, I could barely summon the will to leave her.

The fistula was now extending quite rapidly. Part of her daily equipment that she took the office, was a squirt bottle of scented citrus which she hoped would eliminate the odor that accompanied her. It worked remarkably well. I assured her many times that I could not detect any odor. I know that it eased her mind.

*

A doctor at a clinic Gloria frequented, suggested that she consider Hyperbaric Oxygen Treatment in an effort to retard the growth of the fistula and possibly heal the wound, now a gaping open fissure that extended from one inch above her vagina to two inches below it. The theory of oxygen treatment is that oxygen under pressure applied directly to a wound, will speed the healing. Since Gloria's wound was hardly exposed to any oxygen under present conditions, the treatment really appealed to her. She, now in desperation, agreed to the protocol: twenty sessions of two and a half hours each. Each day for five weeks, while I waited, she was inserted into an airtight plastic cylinder and subjected to a maximum pressure of two and a half atmospheres of pure oxygen (the equivalent in pressure, of being lowered into about seventy feet of seawater). The immediate results looked positive. The fissure looked less angry and seemed to be drying up, and Gloria felt better.

One morning however, we found an unusual, seemingly odorless mucous emerging from the fistula. Following this phenomenon, there no longer appeared any positive progress in the condition of the wound.

Finally, bypassing the doctor's opinions, we decided that the substance emerging from the fissure was indeed feces, and that Gloria's bowel must be ruptured.

I called Stanford Clinic and secured a bed in the Emergency Room for midnight. Hiring a small van, wherein Gloria might lie flat, took half an hour and by 7:pm we were on the road to Stanford.

At night the drive to the clinic seemed interminable, but shortly after midnight, Gloria was admitted to the E.R. A culture of a specimen taken from the fissure, determined that it was indeed, feces.

An examination by the same, but more serious faced, surgeon showed that surgery would have to be performed soon. After clearing her bowels, she went into surgery at 7:am the following day. That same evening at 10:pm I met the surgeon in the waiting room. One look at his face told me all I wanted to know. He told me, in medical terms, that he had removed several inches of decaying bowel, the result of earlier radiation, and blanked the remaining end off. He had also removed her bladder, upon which he had found a cancerous node. Struggling to find the right phrases and vocabulary to tell me, he said that he had done all he could to repair an irreparable condition, but he said that the *cloaca,* the deep fissure between Gloria's legs, was also irreparable: *squamous cancer* cells had infested her pelvic lining and would destroy everything—and take her life.

We saw the surgeon for a few days after the surgery. He explained that the word *Cloaca,* was from an ancient latin word meaning *sewer,* or *drain hole.* The body, it seems, during its miraculous design, developed the lower pelvis into a place where waste bodily fluid drained and became assimilated in bodily functions. In Gloria's case it would appear that the cancer ate a hole in her skin sack, resulting in this terrible open wound.

She remained At Stanford for a further ten days while given all the expert care the clinic offered.

Unable to stand, some good friends of ours, kindly offered their motor home for her return journey home. The drive home for us became four hours of silence interrupted by occasional, carefully selected questions and suggestions. They knew of the surgeons' ultimatum. For my part, I sat by Gloria and held her hand thinking numbly of the days/weeks/months ahead. Inevitably, my thoughts centered on myself. What will I do when she's gone? How am I going to carry on when my best friend in the world is no longer around to talk to me? Several times during the journey, Gloria uttered gasping noises and I knew she was in pain. *Vicodin* was all we had, but that helped although, I myself, hate the stuff.

Dressing her wound *en route,* became excruciating. Recent scars and tenderness must have been almost unbearable for her yet she tried hard not to make us feel like executioners.

A persistent, sharp pain in her groin made it necessary for us to return to Mercy for an x-ray which revealed a fractured pelvic bone. It was digging into the flesh behind her pubis. The doctor who came to examine her said, "Don't worry too much; So long as you keep downward pressure on one end of the bone, against the other, it will knit." I can well remember thinking, how stupid could this man be. He'd seen the wound between her legs and knew her days were numbered, yet he makes a foolish diagnosis like that. ""Thanks Doc, you have been a great comfort," I said.

*

. . . . A hospital-type bed became a new piece of furniture in our living room. Gloria would never climb the stairs to the bedroom again; she was simply too weak.

The last rally she made to save her life was to visit her own oncologist, an experienced, down to earth man who told things as they were. He told her she had about nine months to live and that he would assist in any way he could. He explained that there were a few mixtures of chemo that might attack the squamous carcinoma in her pelvis, and with her consent, he arranged for the mixing and delivery of two or three types of chemo to a nearby clinic where Gloria attended every Monday for about six sessions.

The chemo made no visible affect on her condition, but the *cloaca* grew fast. I changed her, bathed her and changed her dressings and napkins every day except when a hospice nurse was there. She now had to deal with smaller bag into which urine escaped. This proved quite a different operation from dealing with the colostomy: much trickier to handle and therefore more exasperating.

Gloria's oncologist paid a visit to our house. He sat very comfortably next to her and gave us his thoughts. He mentioned a movie called, "The Bucket List" wherein Jack Nicholson, a millionaire, and Morgan Freeman, a modest working man, find themselves next to each other in a cancer ward, each dying of the same affliction. Both are sick and tired of waiting to die. Nicholson comes up with the idea that they pool resources and spend their last days doing everything they may have dreamed of doing, but because of their circumstances at that time, failed to follow their dreams. And that is what they did. They simply left the hospital, purchased all the gear and necessary equipment they would need to travel around the world, and flew to all the 'wonders of the world' until they died.

Poor Gloria was aghast. "Are you serious?" she asked, "I can hardly get from here to the bathroom." And she was right. The fissure between her legs was as much of a deterrent as if she had been shackled with a ball and chain. The idea was brilliant, but the execution not feasible. We thanked the doctor for giving his time to *visit a patient at home.*

Gloria's spiritual condition, her hopes and aspirations, her views of a next life, were just beyond my grasp. I believe they were also beyond her grasp, too. One particular neighbor occasionally came by and would read her short texts from the New Testament. One phrase, or instruction, caught her eye: *"Jesus said, 'ask in my name and you will receive."* I know she was curious and doubtful about things like this that were quoted from the Bible or the New Testament. I later (after her death) found between the pages of a book she had been reading, a piece of yellow foolscap paper: written in various parts of one side were pleas to God to relieve her of this cancer. *Please God, take it away. if you love me, please remove this disease; why, oh, why have I been so afflicted?* And I knew why she was so confused at messages like this that have been gospel-ed around the world for two thousand years and more; I wonder how many times the requests had been fulfilled. But I did not know what she actually believed in—and yet within a few short months, she would be in His presence.

In the Spring of 2009, a true spirit joined us in our daily lives at home: Mercy Hospice. The spirit arrived in form of nurses and a chaplain. Both Gloria and I truly believed that they were sent by the Holy Spirit. We fell in love with them. Each day I would rush to the front door to let either one in. Not only were they superb in their chosen field of medicine, they were incurably bright and buoyant. We looked forward so much each weekday to their arrival. The chaplain, a quiet, sincere man provided me with much needed comfort. Gloria took what he said seriously and asked me many times what my opinion was of what he said about the hereafter, although he did not often refer to death as such.

During the long unbroken vigils at her bedside, I sometimes fantasized that time was somehow bypassing us, and that we had been swept into an eddy, sometimes bumping into 'bubbles' of time, yet finding ourselves back where we were days ago.

She was now on *dilauden,* an opiate:a regulated dose is pumped into her vein keeping her pain-free. She is, however, able to increase the dose in case of need.

In April, when the weather became a bit warmer, Gloria's last locks fell out. Without hesitation she announced that she would buy a wig This would be the last time she would go shopping. Dressing her up with the help of a couple of her colleagues was exciting.

Finding the right wig was hilarious. Now that she had none, she tried on wigs of every description and hue: long blond wigs, long flaming red wigs and all the latest blue wigs. All of her friends wanted to try them on too. You can imagine that the fitting room in the shop became a bubbling boutique. I didn't particularly like the wig she finally picked, an ash-white wig that was kind of piled up, but she did and that is all that mattered.

Her decision to get a headpiece was timely, for quite out of the blue, my nephew, his wife and two daughters arrived from Melbourne, Australia. I had told him in an email of Gloria's condition. He wanted to see her.

Vincent and Gloria took to each other right away. He sat next to her whenever he could. Chris, his wife very soon overcame the shyness and awkwardness some people have talking to a dying person, and she, too chatted away. But the two girls dared not look at Gloria. I'm not sure what it is, but some people can't talk to the dying for fear of somehow upsetting them. After a couple of hours I took Vincent outside and asked him to ask his daughters to forget what embarrassment assailed them and get as close to Gloria as they could. It worked, I am happy to say. Gloria naturally understood their predicament, but was delighted when they came and started telling her about their affairs in Australia. They told her about their boy friends and how they watch 'footie', Australian football. Their broad Australian accent was quite unintelligible to Gloria who relied on Vincent for a translation.

I was very pleased to see that Vincent and Chris were not just talking to Gloria but getting her ear, and she was responding just as she would to her local close friends.

*

The summer of 2009 seemed less oppressive than previous summers. We are fortunate to have a two-storied house which tends to allow the bottom floor to remain cool. I worried a lot about Gloria getting too hot and becoming dehydrated.

In July, her brother Larry and his significant other, Karen came out from Michigan to say goodbye. During this period at the end of her life, when all of Gloria' kin and friends were saying their good bye's, I realized that they would, indeed, never see her again. It struck me that I, too, would have to do the same. And then it occurred to me that my brother, Tom, had died in Australia without a farewell from me. Tom and his son, Vincent, were dead ringers. Seeing Vincent talking so earnestly to Gloria, I had the eeriest sense that it was Tom, my brother, who was saying good-bye, and somehow I made the connection—and bid him *adieu* right there. My nephew and his charming family, left the following day to continue their tour of the Southern States.

*

While Larry and Karen were here, Gloria perked up and there was much laughter, especially when they reminisced about their childhood together in the suburbs of Detroit. She also got him to organize her still-active client files. When she cleared her office out about ten months ago, about three-hundred files were un-alphabetically placed in filing boxes and stored in our garage. With Karen's help, he alphabetized and tabulated all of them into eight filing boxes, a job that took them four or five days.

Before they returned to Michigan, they helped Gloria arrange a small party for my birthday on July 28. A select group of her closest friends gathered around her bed and sang to me, and we ate hotdogs and beans, one of my favorites, followed by a cream covered carrot cake.

I watched Gloria throughout the festivities. Once in a while our eyes would meet and I wondered what she was thinking. I wanted to go over and hug her, and tell her that everything was going to be okay

It was the beginning of August and we knew that we are in the last phase of her life.

I sense that I am in the limbo of a life that will soon dramatically change. We seldom ever ventured into that no-mans-land called the 'hereafter.'

A spiritual group made up of her closest colleagues, and me, met twice a week at her beside. We discussed the writings in "A Course in Miracles," by Helen Schucman *et all,* and suggestions made by Gary Renard in his book, "The Disappearance of the Universe." A part of Renard's book is fantasy, but many sections of it, depending on ones mind-set regarding the contents of the Bible, make a great deal of sense, especially when the Bible talks about the creation of man, the Garden of Eden and the departure of

Adam and Eve from the Garden of Eden.

As the Dog Days rage outside, Gloria gets weaker. She barely weighs one-hundred pounds, but still struggles do for herself. One morning, as I bend over to help her, she put her arms around my neck and whispers. "I can't do this any more, Peter," and I know that she has reached the very end of her tether. Until that moment, a part of my psyche had refused to brook the idea that Gloria was dying and had but a short time to live. He voice has become softer and I am obliged to listen carefully to her. She now has a constant inflow of *dilauded* to quell the pain. But that narcotic, no longer potent and has some painful and frightening side effects: severe muscle spasms.

I call Hospice and describe what is happening. The nurse arrives within the hour with another drug and pump. It is called *versed* ;it is an anesthetic, which calmed her immediately.

One of our dear friends and constant companion, Robin, arrives to do the night watch, just after the hospice nurse leaves. I fall asleep and am woken at 2:15. Robin is saying "She's gone, Peter." I knew exactly what she meant, but the full significance didn't immediately register. In a stupor, I get up and gaze at her dear face. Dare I make sure? I pick up her hand, still supple, but cool; I touch her lips, soft and smooth. I ask

Robin, "you are sure?" She nods. And then Igo back to Gloria and straighten a wisp of hairThe chemo had failed to destroy, and remove her rings and necklace.

Robin has called hospice with the news, and I sit by her until the coroner and hospice arrive.

I collect clothes I have chosen for her to wear, and Robin and I dress her in a silk blouse and worsted pants. She looks beautiful lying there, calm and serene, her lips slightly parted. Feeing as though I am acting in some terrible, epic, tragic play, I cross her lovely hands over her chest just below her bosom—beautiful.

I ask the coroner's men not to put her in a body bag. They explain the law, but meet me half way by leaving her face and chest uncovered so that the rest of the world can also say good-bye.

I watch them take her away, and as the front door closes I let out a wail of despair. My heroine has gone.

I am standing
At the end of
A bridge
To nowhere.

*   *   *

Epilogue

Five months have passed. The ready tears have almost ceased to flow but the dull ache persists in my chest. The telephone, a machine whose harsh insistence I have come to dread, rings less often. With a catch in my voice I explain that she is no longer with us—and feel empty again.

Another week has gone by and I have done nothing: not ventured outside and ignored telephone calls. I well know that inaction will do me harm. I have decided to redecorate the two spare bedrooms upstairs, and lay hardwood floors, repaint the walls and get some new drapes. I will start soon.

Searching through Gloria's things, I found a small book, "Healing after Loss" by Martha Whitmore Hickman. Leafing through the pages, I found a piece by Daphne du Maurier, which I found comforting: *"As the months pass and the seasons change, something of tranquility descends, and although the well-remembered footstep will not sound again, nor the voice call from the room beyond, there seems to be about one in the air an atmosphere of love; a living presence . . . its is as though shared in some indefinable manner the freedom and peace, even at times the joy, of another world where there is no pain . . . the feeling is simply there, pervading all thought, all action. When Christ the Healer said, 'blessed are they that mourn, for they shall be comforted' He must have meant just this."*

I knew immediately what du Maurier was referring to because I had already experienced some of the same sensations. After sitting, sadly thinking about the future, I would get the feeling that Gloria was there with me. A wave of comfort would envelope me, and I would feel good for a day or so. Often I would become distressed and very lonely, and would ask her to help. She never failed. I later found out that she had helped some of close colleagues in the same way.

Knowing that Grief Groups can be of great benefit, but contrary to my normal "I can do it myself" attitude, I spent many fruitful hours at Mercy Grief Group. To my delight the same padre who had visited us at home, was the counselor. Listening to men and women of all ages, sometimes tearfully, sometimes bravely, tell of the deaths of their parents, husbands or mothers, gave me courage and some wisdom. I met them a few months later and asked them what they did to keep busy. Their answers were quite simple: walking the river trail: exercising and going to parties.

I would like to express my thanks to that padre, the mediator; always so gentle and firm. He had a vocabulary and a collection of metaphors that described and bracketed every mood and phase of the mourners' early emotional onset.

After two months, I left the group and spent my time working on the upstairs rooms. I could not venture into the garden without some distress, for the last time Gloria was in the garden, sitting in her wheelchair under our white oak, was in mid-spring when a group of neighbors had instituted a weeding party. I think of her sitting forlornly, watching her friends performing yet another kind act for her. I know how much she wanted to join them, but was too weak. She did, however give them a radiant smile.

The garden is once more hers. I cleared a small spot around her statue of Buddha and placed her ashes. The statue guards the spot. Charlie, our Springer, is buried five feet to her left under a small statuette of two nymphs on a garden swing. Charlie died two weeks after his mistress. Every day of her sickness, he spent on the floor next to her bed. The morning she died, he moved to a place next to the French doors that lead into the garden.

Every now and then, perhaps twice a week, I make a sortie into the garden to tidy the graves and pull a few weeds. I had promised myself that come summers-end, I would have the garden looking 'S*hipshape and Bristol Fashion':* but all I have done is place more flowers in the rockery. I will often sit by her Buddha for an hour and meditate.

It is the closest place, in my world, that I can get to her.

*   *   *

Remembering my friend Gloria

Marcella Thompson

*

Gloria was a quiet complicated woman. Thinking about her, brings up a range of emotions as deep and complex as the woman I am remembering. Gloria had a native clear—sightedness. She understood things at a deep level, and fought passionately to make sense of things. This is perhaps why she made such an amazing psychotherapist.

Gloria was also a great referral source for many therapists. We sent clients to her with addiction problems, and while she never made that process easy for them, if they stayed with her,they could once again reclaim their own life while building a new path. Gloria was able to simplify some of life's most difficult problems, and allow people, once again to stand in their own truth and face life head on. Then the day came that Gloria was faced to do this in a way that shattered us all: she had to face the end of life. She was not ready; we were not ready to let her go. I remember the day she so bravely said, "Dying is just part of life's process." I knew then that she had made peace with death.

Losing our friend changed the lives of us all. Her circle of friends remained loyal, and at her bedside until the end. I believe she always knew we were there; for that reason, Gloria died a good death. Sometimes I wonder is she didn't stay just for us. It was hard for her to leave Peter and the life she knew; but in the end she was ready—and she died admirably, peacefully and without pain, into her next level of expression.

I miss my friend, but not a day goes by that her memory fails to visit me. I see her in the many gifts she made me that adorn my home and office. At work, when I open my computer hutch, her picture is there to remind me that life is not predictable and often much shorter than we expected. Gloria reminds me to live well, so that when my time comes to leave this earth, I too, may die well. Until we meet again, my friend . . .

Ω

Remembering Gloria

DaLene Forester.

I had the distinct honor of having a friend, a mentor, a sister and a colleague named Gloria.

Gloria came into my life as a Clinical Supervisor, became my business partner, and then my best friend and confidant; I feel she still is. I miss her more than words can tell.

I hear her laughter in my ears, and her voice, sometimes more than I want.

What made Gloria such a phenomenal therapist? As much as she would hate to admit it, to me she seemed to fall in love with her clients. Gloria was seriously aware of ethics and making sure that nothing non-ethical ever crossed her desk. She would never have thought it ethical to say that she 'loved' her clients, but in a way, she did.—and they got healed.

She and I shared so many thoughts that we could have entire conversations without ever finishing a sentence, but we knew exactly what we were talking about, much to the bewilderment of our spouses and present company.

When I went through a particularly bad time in my life, Gloria was there, a strong and loving friend. She listened but rarely gave advice. We walked and talked together every day. She would ask me how well I was doing, supported my grieving process, but for the most part refrained from telling me what to do. Occasionally she would give me counsel, the full impact of which, I did not recognize until later in my life, after she became ill.

My most treasured memory is her once saying very quietly, "you are a good friend."

It was, for me, the highest honor I could receive from the very person whom I considered 'my best friend.' During some of my drab days, I miss her humor and her delightfully contagious laugh: when Gloria laughed, everyone laughed.

Ω

.